HOLIDAY PUPPETS

Lothrop, Lee & Shepard Company

NEW YORK

LAURA ROSS
HOLIDAY PUPPETS

DRAWINGS AND DIAGRAMS BY
Frank and Laura Ross

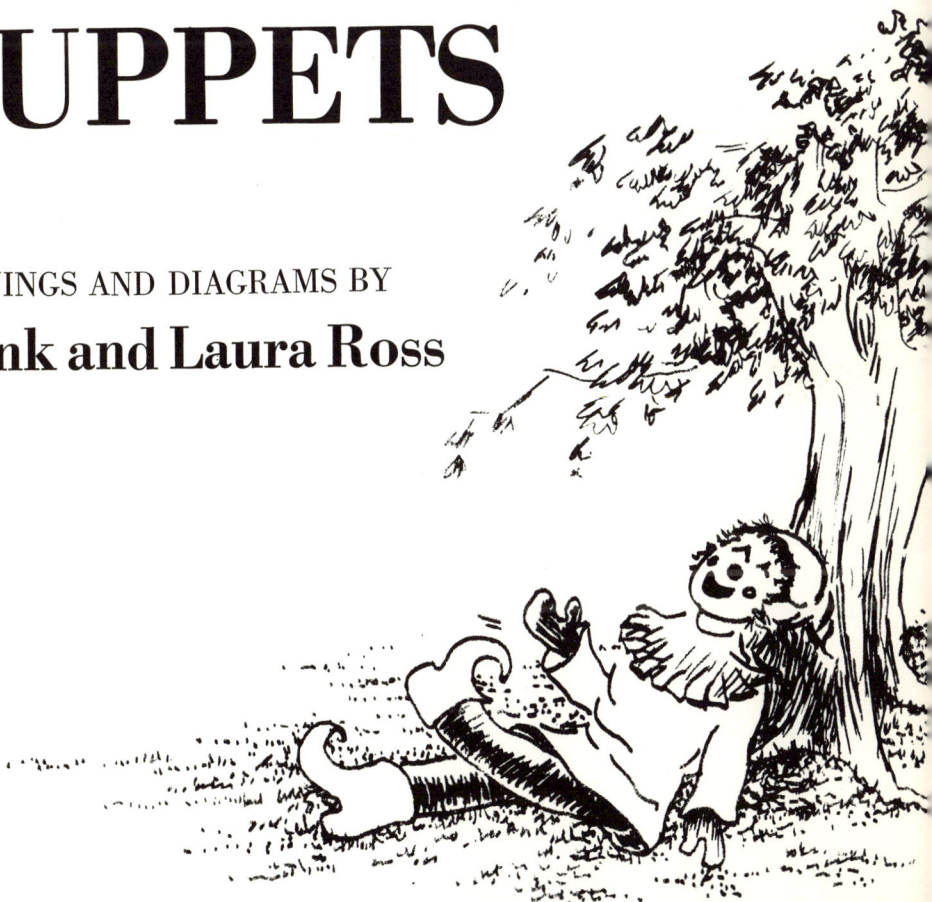

1/18/75

1 2 3 4 5 78 77 76 75 74

Library of Congress Cataloging in Publication Data

Ross, Laura
    Holiday puppets.

    SUMMARY: Instructions for making puppets from a variety of materials. Includes holiday plays to cast them in.
    1. Puppets and puppet-plays—Juvenile literature. [1. Puppets and puppet-plays]
I. Ross, Frank Xavier (date) illus. II. Title.
PN1972.R592   791.5'38   73-17720
ISBN 0-688-41556-3
ISBN 0-688-51556-8 (lib. bdg.)

Other books by Laura Ross:

FINGER PUPPETS: *Easy to Make, Fun to Use*
PUPPET SHOWS: *Using Poems and Stories*
HAND PUPPETS: *How to Make and Use Them*

This book is fondly dedicated
to the gracious, helpful librarians
of the Rogers Memorial Library
in Southampton

Photographs courtesy of George Dec Studios

CONTENTS

HOLIDAY PUPPETS

FOREWORD

This book is for children and for adults who work with children. It shows you how to make a variety of puppets for special holiday plays and stories, which are also included. The puppets are made of natural and man-made materials, such as corn husks, straw, apples, paper, and styrofoam. The dimensions given in the text are those I used. However, you may prefer to make your puppets smaller or larger.

I shall tell you how to make one puppet for each play and make suggestions for decorating the other, similarly constructed, puppets in the play. In some plays, you will learn how to make several puppets, because each one is constructed differently.

The ideas in this book are just suggestions. You can think of ways to make and decorate your own puppets, using other materials, if you like, but following these basic directions.

LAURA ROSS

13

INTRODUCTION

Before planning puppets for plays or stories, try to decide on your approach. First, are you making puppets for the fun of making them and then writing a play to fit the puppets? This will depend on the materials you have on hand or want to use. Such materials as scraps of wood or wooden spools from the sewing box often suggest a puppet character. It is fun to write your own play for these puppets.

Are you making puppets for a specific play? If you want to use a particular play or story for a puppet show, you must create a puppet to fit the story. These puppets can be imaginative, but they must be appropriate for the story.

A certain amount of thought and planning always go into making puppets. However, once you've decided on the type of puppet you'll make, work on it spontaneously. When possible, exaggerate and stylize your puppets. Remember, they are not dolls but characters.

No matter what type of puppet you use, try to keep the dialogue and action of the puppet show spontaneous. Elaborate and change the mood each time you play out the story. Keep rehearsals to a minimum, and do not worry about making mistakes. The important thing in a puppet show is to give a creative and spontaneous performance.

The plays in this book are suggested for holiday puppet shows. You need not use them. You can write your own holiday play or find one you prefer. In any event, be sure the play is interesting, and has suspense and action.

To stage these holiday puppet plays, or to make papier-maché puppets, read my book entitled, *Hand Puppets: How to Make and Use Them*. Be a magician and see how many different holiday puppets and puppet shows you can create.

15

BASIC MATERIALS

Do you know that you can make exciting puppets with such household materials as wrapping paper, newspaper, and Q-tips? Also, paper, cardboard, cloth, wallpaper, crayons, and odds and ends are ideal for making puppets.

You need not buy every item you use. Keep a scrap box for buttons, sequins, ribbon, braid, feathers, scraps of printed fabric, discarded dresses, blouses, and nylon stockings, old sheets and pillow cases, colored felt, rickrack, empty spools of thread, paper doilies, and other household items. Any material that can be put together and made to move can become a puppet.

Scraps of wood can be picked up at the lumberyard for the asking. Construction and drawing paper, dowels, glue, and Scotch tape are inexpensive and available at neighborhood shops.

To use materials, you need certain techniques, which are explained here. Once you know how to handle the materials correctly you can combine them and invent your own designs and shapes for puppets.

This book includes puppets that have been made with all sorts of materials. You need not make yours the same way. There are many different ways to put together materials to create puppets. You are the magician who can create people, animals, and birds that move at your command.

Paper

Of all the different materials used for making puppets, paper is the most versatile. It can be rolled, folded, curled, twisted, and bent.

All paper is made with vertical and horizontal fibers, like fabric. Some kinds of paper have a certain amount of rag content; others consist only of wood fibers.

Always tear or fold paper with the grain going up and down. To find the grain, tear a small piece. When you tear with the grain, the paper will tear evenly and straight. Tearing against the grain will give you a ragged, uneven tear. This is important to know when you fold construction paper, because the paper will not fold smoothly against the grain and may even crack. Rolling, bending, creasing, scoring, and curling paper should also be done with the grain of the paper.

Many different kinds of paper are useful for making puppets. Some are: construction paper, Bristol drawing paper, poster board, railroad board, crepe paper, gift wrap, wallpaper, foil paper, colored cellophane paper, newsprint, paper towels, tissue and typing paper, manila and craft-paper bags, and cardboard.

Aluminum foil:

Has a very special use because of its shine and manageability. It is especially good for covering a milk bottle or container to construct a robot. Try costuming the three kings for a Christmas story with it.

Bristol drawing paper:

Comes in white only and is especially nice as a smooth, medium-weight paper for basic construction. It usually comes in pads of different ply for drawing purposes. A two-ply weight is good for constructing basic shapes. Most of the animals constructed for the Easter play can be made of this paper.

Cardboard:

Very heavy paper and excellent for making simple puppet stages. It can also be used as a board for the push-puppets in this book.

Colored cellophane-paper:
Strips of cellophane are excellent for making hair.

Construction paper:
Medium weight and firm enough to use for a basic construction as well as for decorations. It comes in assorted colors and smaller and larger sheets. A large sheet will enable you to work with larger as well as smaller pieces by cutting the paper to size. The variety of colors will suggest over-all color schemes.

Craft-paper bags and manila paper:
Brown, strong, and firm, these are suitable for heavy-duty forms.

Crepe paper:
Resembles fabric in texture and is flexible. It readily responds to whatever you do to it. It will stretch little or much. It will fold and is soft enough to shape with your fingers. Remember to cut it with the grain. It comes in a variety of colors and is used mostly for decorating, draping, and for making hair.

Gift-wrap paper and wallpaper:
Fun to use because their prints and designs are so colorful and decorative. These are effective for costumes of various kinds. Whenever you find unusual pieces, put them in your scrap box.

Newspaper:
Good for making practice patterns before cutting the material you plan to use. It can also be used as a stuffing for some of the puppets. It may be shredded for various other purposes.

Paper towels:
Good stuffing, especially for discarded nylon stockings, with which you can make puppet heads.

Poster board:
A heavy construction paper that comes in a large sheet and

various colors. It must be scored with a sharp tool before it is bent; otherwise it will crack.

Railroad board:

A heavier type of construction paper than poster board, it is used primarily for very heavy-duty constructions. It comes in a large size and is colored on one side only. It also must be scored.

Tissue and typing paper:

Useful for lightweight constructions like birds and insects.

Save pieces of interesting paper. The more you collect the more you will appreciate the variety of colors and textures that can be used together to create objects that are rich in contrast.

WORKING METHODS
Basic Shapes

Once you have a good collection of paper, try making different forms and shapes with it. Many objects can be made with three-dimensional shapes, either by themselves or in combinations that can be used as puppets.

When making puppets with shapes, think of the structural forms of the figures. Then decide what shapes will best describe the figures. A cone or cylinder can be part of a body. Add another cone or cylinder, and you have a body with a head. After the basic shapes have been decided on, emphasize the shapes to make them interesting, without worrying about details. The omission of details sometimes improves the structural design of the work.

You can use milk cartons, oatmeal boxes, cream cartons, and towel and toilet-paper tubes. You can also make your own shapes with paper.

Most three-dimensional forms start with a flat piece of paper. It could be a square, in which all sides are equal, or a rectangle, with two equal sides.

The basic shapes described in this section include only those used in the text.

Cylinder:
The simplest three-dimensional shape to make. Roll a strip of paper of the desired length and width, closing the edges. This becomes a tube with a round opening at the top and bottom. A long, wide strip of paper makes a long, wide tube when closed. A short, narrow strip, makes a short narrow tube. Before closing the edges, roll the strip of paper over the edge of

Cylinder

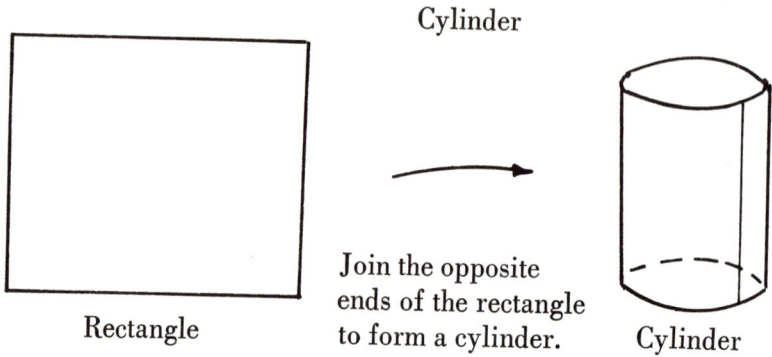

Rectangle

Join the opposite
ends of the rectangle
to form a cylinder.

Cylinder

a table to curve it. Let one edge overlap the other about ¼ inch and glue them together. Hold each edge with a paper clip until the glue is dry.

The head, arms, torso, and legs of a human figure can be constructed with cylinders of various sizes. You can also make animals, such as a horse, giraffe, lion, and others.

Circle:

A circle is another basic shape. To make a circle, tie one end of a piece of string to a pencil. The length of the string will depend on how large a circle you will need. The longer the string, the larger the circle. The shorter the string, the smaller the circle. This length is called the radius of a circle. With one finger, hold the free end of the string against the center of a piece of paper. This will be the center of the circle. With

Tie one end of a string to a pencil.
Hold the free end of the string
on the paper with one finger,
and make a circle with the
pencil in the other hand.
Cut out the circle with scissors.

Circle

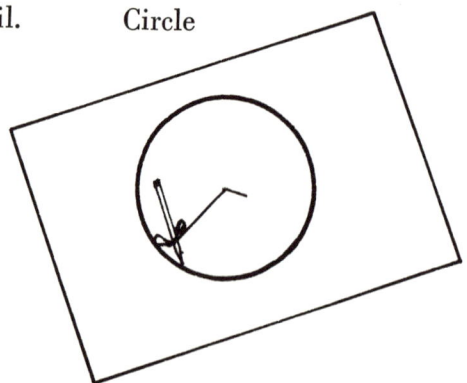

the pencil in your other hand, pull the string straight out and circumscribe a circle. Cut out the circle with scissors.

Cone:

A shape that's frequently used to make puppets, a cone is made from a whole circle or part of a circle, and is pointed at the top and broad at the base. The size of a cone depends on the size of the circle and also on whether it is made from a full circle, a three-quarter circle, a half circle, or a quarter circle.

Making a Cone From a Circle

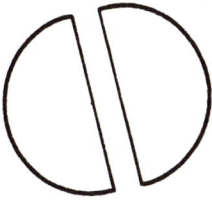

Cut circle in half. Roll the half circle
to form a cone. Overlap the edges
of the cone and
glue the sides together.

If a full circle is used, cut a slit from the edge of the circle to its exact center. Overlap the two cut sides and seal them with glue or Scotch tape. The size of this cone can also be controlled by the size of the overlap. The larger the overlap, the narrower the cone. The smaller the overlap, the broader the cone. The three-quarter circle makes a smaller cone; the half circle, a smaller cone; and the quarter circle, the smallest. Close the back of the cone with glue or Scotch tape. If glue is used, the overlap must be held in position with a paper clip until the glue is dry. Experiment, making different-sized cones with parts of circles of various sizes.

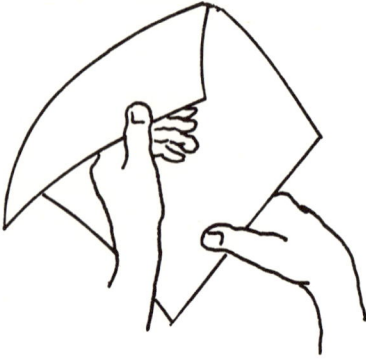

Hold the right corner of
the rectangle-shaped paper
with the right hand.
Hold the left corner
with the left hand.

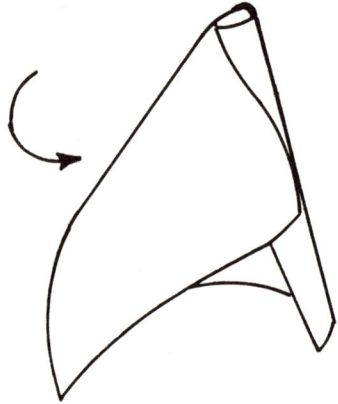

Roll the left corner
down and around the
right corner until the
cone is the desired width.

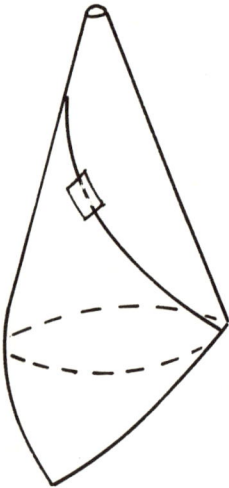

Close with tape.
Cut off excess paper at the bottom.

Another way to make a cone is to start with a rectangular piece of paper. The larger the rectangle, the larger the cone will be. Pick up the lower-right corner of the short side of the rectangle with your right hand. Then pick up the upper left corner of the opposite short side with your left hand. Roll the paper down and around your right hand until you make a cone of the desired width. Tape or glue the edge down. This can be varied by changing the size of the overlap. The smaller the overlap, the wider the cone opening at the top and bottom. The greater the overlap, the narrower the cone opening at the top and bottom. With scissors, trim off the bottom to make a circular opening. The base will stand upright.

The first method requires a larger piece of paper for a large cone and the size of opening at the top and bottom are limited. The second method requires less paper for a large cone and you can control the size of the opening at the top and bottom.

Practice making these basic forms with different kinds of paper. You will notice that different paper will respond differently to some fastening methods. For example, very thin paper, like tissue, will tear if it is stapled together. Thick paper may crack and weaken when folded. The finished product of those may need to be reenforced at the fold with Scotch tape. Very thick paper will not roll well into a cone.

You must know what your paper can or cannot do well. This, of course, will take practice and experiment.

Paper Techniques

You need certain skills to work with paper. These are acquired through experience, and sometimes by making mistakes. However, if you know some techniques of working with paper beforehand, such as cutting, folding, bending, scoring, and curling, you may make fewer mistakes. The techniques mentioned here are those used in the text. They are not rules but suggestions.

Cutting:

A rod puppet can be made by drawing a figure on stiff paper, cutting it out, and attaching it to a rod. Use large scissors for heavy, stiff paper. Use a smaller scissors for thin and delicate paper. For narrow intricate curves, manicure scissors are best.

Folding:

Fold thin paper by making a sharp crease with your fingers. A flat figure will stand up if you draw it on a piece of folded paper. Draw a half figure on the fold. Cut around it, but do not cut the fold. When the sheet is opened, the two sides will be exactly alike and attached at the top or side. It can stand by itself or with tabs at the bottom, which are attached to a push-board. This becomes a push-puppet that can be moved about on the stage.

Scoring:

To bend medium and heavy paper, you must first score it. If it is not scored, it will crack at the fold. To score, draw a line on the drawing where you want to fold it. Hold the ruler over the line. Groove the surface of the paper with the point of a nail file, knife blade, or scissors, using the ruler as a guide. If the paper is very heavy, do this twice. Make sure you do not cut through the paper. Cut only the surface fibers.

After it is scored, the paper will not resist the fold, which will be clean, neat, and exactly where you want it. Scoring is necessary for folding three-dimensional shapes. It also permits you to make a nose with three planes, the front and two sides. A flat drawn figure can also be given a three-dimensional effect if you score it down the center. Bend it along the score line, and the figure will stand upright on a base. Attach the figure to a wooden board, and you have a push-puppet.

Curling:

Paper can be curled with a blade of scissors or a knife, a round pencil, or the edge of the table.

Cut the strip of paper to be curled. Hold one end between the thumb and first finger. Hold the scissor blade or knife in the other hand with the sharp edge up. Hold the top end of the paper between your thumb and the blade. Pull the blade firmly from the top end of the strip of paper to the bottom. Now you have a piece of curled paper.

When using a pencil instead of a blade, follow the same procedure.

To run a strip of paper over the edge of a table, hold one end between the thumb and first finger of one hand. Hold the other end between the same two fingers of the other hand. Start at the lower end and pull the strip down over the edge of the table.

Curled paper is excellent for making puppets' hair and eyelashes, and for feathers.

Pleating:

Paper can be pleated to form fan-shaped constructions. Start with a piece of paper and make a fold at one end as wide as desired. Reverse the paper and make another fold of the same width as the first. Keep folding forward and back until you reach the end of the paper. Gather it at one end and tie it with a string or staple it to hold. Pleats can be used for birds' wings and tails, puppets' skirts and collars, and decorations.

Cat-stairs:

A very decorative paper zigzag construction is the cat-stairs. To make it, start with two strips of paper of the same length and width. Place one end of one strip on top of the end of the second strip at right angles to make a square corner. Fasten the two ends with a stapler or glue. Fold one strip over the other, keeping the folds square. Do this until you reach the end. Fasten the two ends as you did at the beginning. Stretch it out, and now you have an accordionlike flexible construction. It is decorative and can be effectively used for a puppet's arms and legs, for a cat's tail, and for a jack-in-the-box.

Template:

A template, like a pattern, is a guide with which to outline forms. It is made by tracing a drawing and cutting around it. Then it is superimposed an another piece of paper, held down, and traced. The new drawing is then cut out and used as needed. This technique sometimes saves time.

Tracing Directions

1. Place a piece of thin white typing paper over the drawing in the book, letting the paper extend beyond the edges of the book.

2. Fasten the tracing paper to the work table with Scotch or masking tape.

3. Trace the drawing, but do not press too hard or you will cut through the paper with your pencil point.

4. Trace all solid and dotted lines. Dotted lines indicate folding or internal cutting lines.

5. When you have finished, remove the paper from the book and cut around the solid lines.

6. Some drawings in this book are for only one half of the pattern. To make a full-sized pattern, transfer the tracing to another sheet of paper. Place the traced pattern on the fold of a doubled piece of paper. Tape or pin the traced pattern and the sheet of paper together. Cut around the traced pattern, but do not cut the fold. Remove the tape or pins and open the new pattern to its full size.

Follow these first six steps only when you are making paper patterns. To transfer a drawing to construction paper, follow the first four steps and the following:

7. Remove the paper from the book. Turn it over to its reverse side. Place it on a large piece of scrap paper.

8. With the flat side of a soft pencil, shade over all the lines.

9. Turn it right-side up again.

10. Place it over the construction paper or cardboard.

11. Fasten the two firmly together with a small piece of Scotch or masking tape.

12. With your pencil, retrace the whole drawing on the construction paper or cardboard.

13. Remove the tracing paper and check your drawing against the book. If any lines have been omitted, draw them in.

14. Cut along all solid lines with scissors.

15. Before folding dotted lines, score them lightly with the point of a nail file or scissors. When dotted lines are to be cut, the directions in the text will tell you so.

29

LINCOLN'S BIRTHDAY

Young Abe Wrestles Armstrong

LAURA ROSS

Characters:
Denton Orffut, general-store manager
customer
Abraham Lincoln, a clerk
Jack Armstrong, a strong man
gang of Armstrong's men

Properties:
counter
shelves with grocery items
barrels
fabric
bonnets

Act I

Narrator (*from behind a closed curtain*): In the town of New
   Salem, Illinois, Denton Orffut bought a plot of land for ten
   dollars. He and young Abe built a log cabin on it. This
   became the new general store, with Lincoln as chief clerk
   and postmaster. It was a day in the summer of 1831.

At Curtain Rise:
The interior of a general country store with a counter. Behind
the counter are shelves filled with food products. In front of

30

the counter are small barrels of foodstuff. On the counter are small bolts of calico prints, bonnets, and other goods. Orffut is standing behind the counter, and a customer is in front of it.

Customer: I'll have a side of bacon, Denton. A pound of sugar, a pound of flour. By the way, this clerk of yours. Never saw him hereabouts before. Is he new?

Orffut: You might say so.

Customer: Is he a good worker? He seems a mite slow to me at times.

Orffut (*with much enthusiasm*): A good worker? The best! Why, when he chopped wood to build this cabin, you'd say three men were working. He was so fast. He has brains too. He knows more than any man in the United States. Some day he will be President of these United States. Mark my words. He can also outrun, outlift, outwrestle, and throw down any man in Sangamon County.

Customer: You don't mean to include Jack Armstrong, do you? He's the strongest man in town for miles around. He can lick any man, if not by fair means, then by foul. You know that, Orffut. No one has put him down.

Orffut: I mean Armstrong too. Abe can put him down quicker than a swish from a raccoon's tail!

Customer: You don't say! Would you care to make a bet on that?

Orffut: I'll bet you ten dollars that Abe can throw Armstrong any day!

Customer: You have a bet! (*Curtain*)

Act II

Narrator (*from behind a drawn curtain*): Orffut's boast about Lincoln soon gets around, especially at the saloon near Orffut's store. Soon bets of all kinds are taken, from money to jackknives, and a contest is arranged between Armstrong and young Lincoln. Sports fans from fifty miles around come to see the match.

At Curtain Rise:

Outside the general store, a crowd, including Orffut and the customer, stands around a central clearing, where the contestants are to wrestle. Soon, Armstrong enters and a shout of hurrahs are heard from his gang. Armstrong struts up and down, showing off. Lincoln enters. Armstrong stops to look at him.

Armstrong (*with scorn*): Abe, where are your muscles? I'm gonna throw you, Stringbean!

Lincoln (*speaking slowly*): Oh, I have a few muscles, Jack. You will see. Don't count your chicks before they hatch. (Armstrong and Lincoln wrestle for quite a while, first one appears to be the victor, then the other. Armstrong's gang cheers him when he seems to be victorious, and then Lincoln's friends cheer when Lincoln has the advantage.)

Armstrong (*impatiently*): Wrestle, Abe, wrestle! Are you afraid?

Lincoln (*with a drawl*): Pretty soon, Jack. Pretty soon you'll be out of wind and I'll put you down quicker than a wink.

Armstrong (*rushes at Lincoln, butts him in the stomach and fools him by stamping on his foot*): There, how do you like that, Abe?

Lincoln (*with a cry of pain and an angry shout*): Stomping on my foot wasn't fair, Jack. Now I will have to give you a lesson. (Lincoln lifts Armstrong off the ground, then, shaking him like a dust rag a few times, slams him hard to the ground on his back.)

Armstrong's gang (*rushing at Lincoln and shouting*): You can't do that to Jack. Now we're gonna show *you* Abe.

32

Lincoln (*facing them quickly*): Try it! I'm ready for you!

Armstrong (*getting up and pushing his way to the front of his gang and standing beside Lincoln*): Just a minute fellows! Abe won the match fair and square. He's the best fellow that ever broke into this settlement. *He belongs!*

Crowd (*shouting and cheering*): Yes, yes, he belongs! He belongs! He's not only the best wrestler, but he has brains and he's honest too. Three cheers for honest Abe! Hurrah! Hurrah! Hurrah for Abe Lincoln! (*Curtain closes.*)

Lincoln Puppet

Materials:

poster board or Bristol board
rigid, thin wire, 18 inches long
thin rod, 12 inches long
two paper fasteners
scissors, preferably manicure scissors
tracing paper
pencil
Elmer's Glue-All

Directions:

1. Trace Figures 1 to 5 (see Tracing Directions). Cut them out and make templates from them (see Paper Techniques).
2. With the point of sharp scissors, pierce holes in the places marked x in the drawing at Numbers 1, 2, 3, 4, 5, 6, 7, and 8.
3. Hold right and left arms at Number 1 on each side of the shoulder, and attach arms at Numbers 3 and 4 to this point with a paper fastener. The head of the fastener should face you.
4. Glue the end of the holding rod to the back of the tilted body. Hold it in place and allow it to dry.

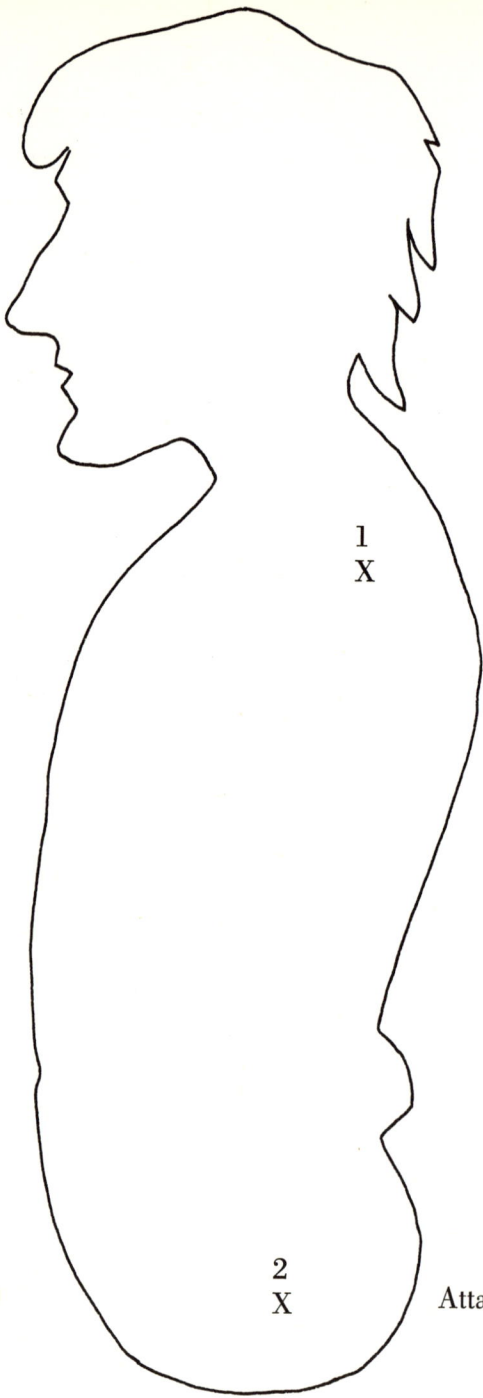

Lincoln

Figure 1

1
X   Attach arms at x.

2
X   Attach legs at x.

Trace and cut out.

34

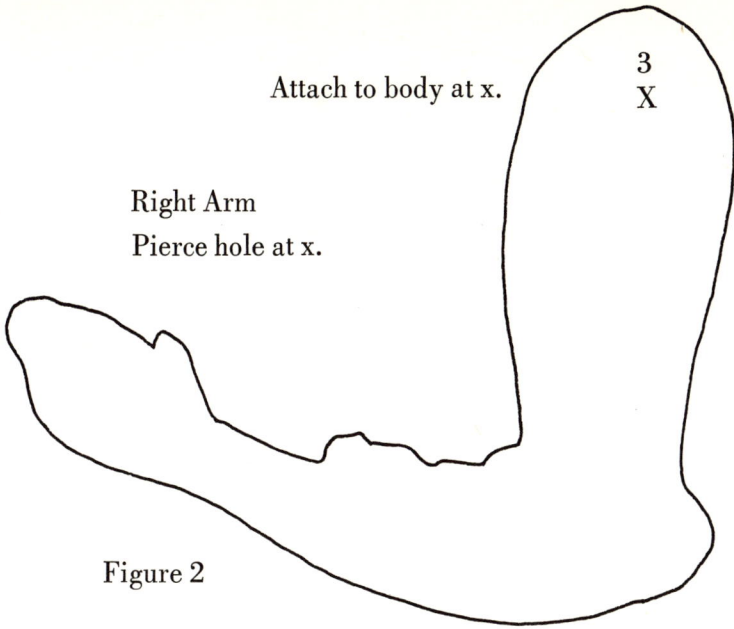

Attach to body at x.

Right Arm
Pierce hole at x.

Figure 2

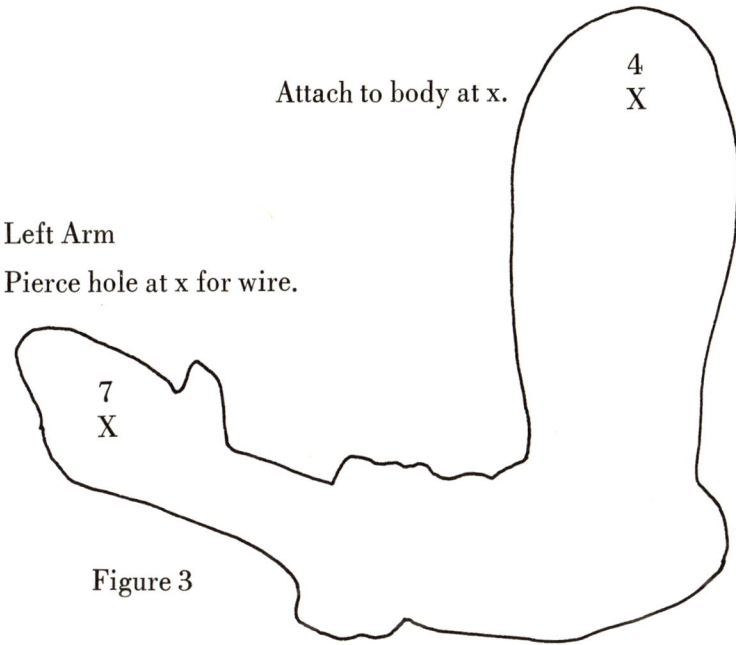

Attach to body at x.

Left Arm
Pierce hole at x for wire.

Figure 3

35

Attach to body at x.

Right Leg

Pierce hole at x.

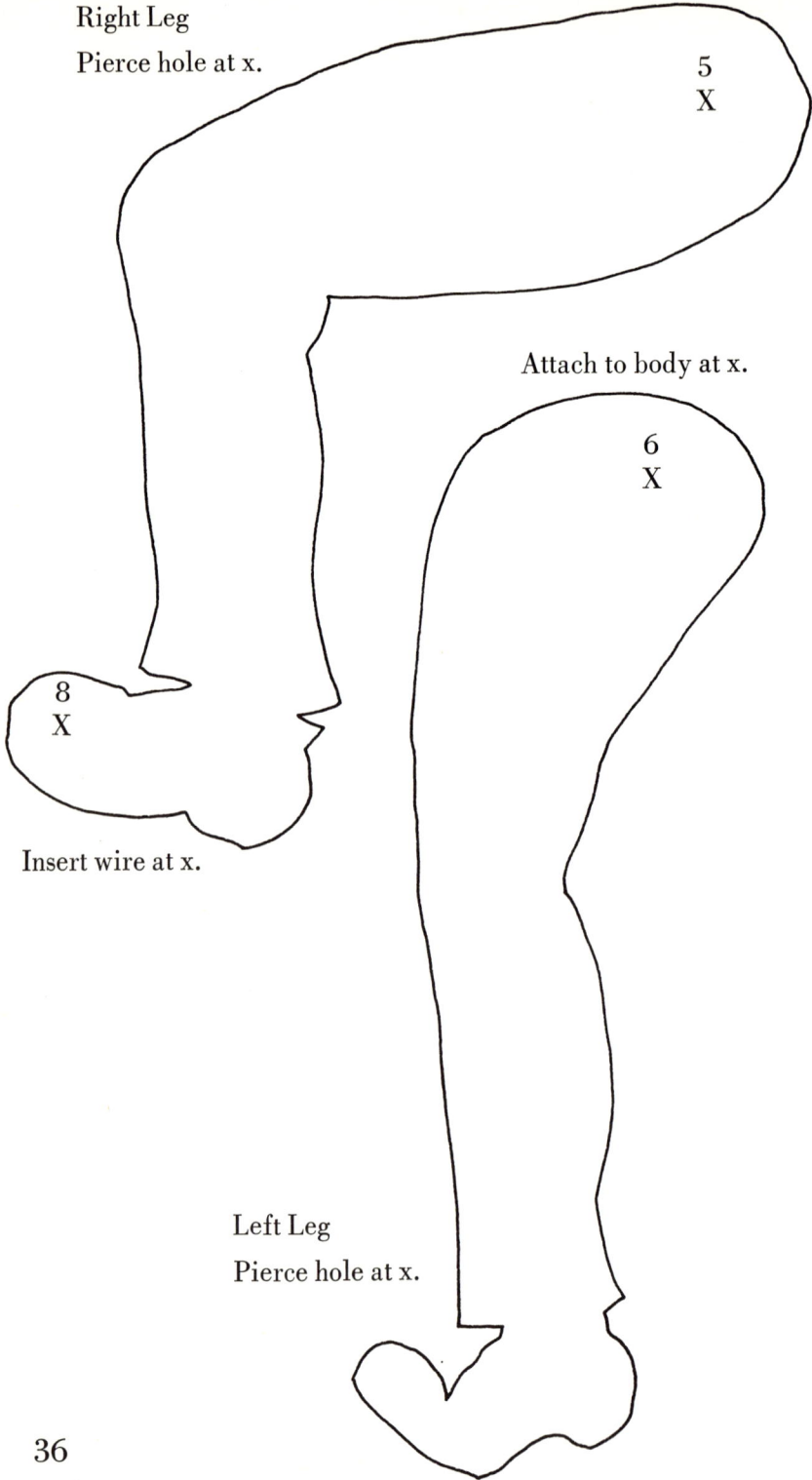

5
X

Attach to body at x.

6
X

8
X

Insert wire at x.

Left Leg

Pierce hole at x.

36

5. Attach legs at Numbers 5 and 6 to Number 2 with a paper fastener, placing one leg on each side of the body. Be sure the holding rod is between the right leg and the body.

6. Position the arms as illustrated in Figure 6 and hold them in place with masking tape on the reverse side.

7. Bend one end of the control wire. Insert the other end through the front of the right foot at Number 8. Insert the bent end through the back of the left hand at Number 7, and pull the loop down securely.

Now young Abe is ready to go into action!

Suggestions for Other Puppets in the Play:
1. Make Armstrong the same way, using a different outline to distinguish him from Abe. Armstrong was much heavier and broader.

2. Make stationary rod puppets to represent the spectators and Armstrong's friends and hold one in each hand. Move the rod when necessary.

Holding the Rod Puppet for Action:
1. Hold the holding rod in one hand and the control wire in the other, with the front of the puppet facing the audience.

2. Move the control wire up and down as you move the holding rod from left to right. This will make the puppet look as though he is wrestling.

Production Notes

Scenery and Properties:
To simplify the interior of a general country store, you may paint shelves with food products on a backdrop instead of making real shelves. Small items, such as bonnets and other goods, are on the counter.

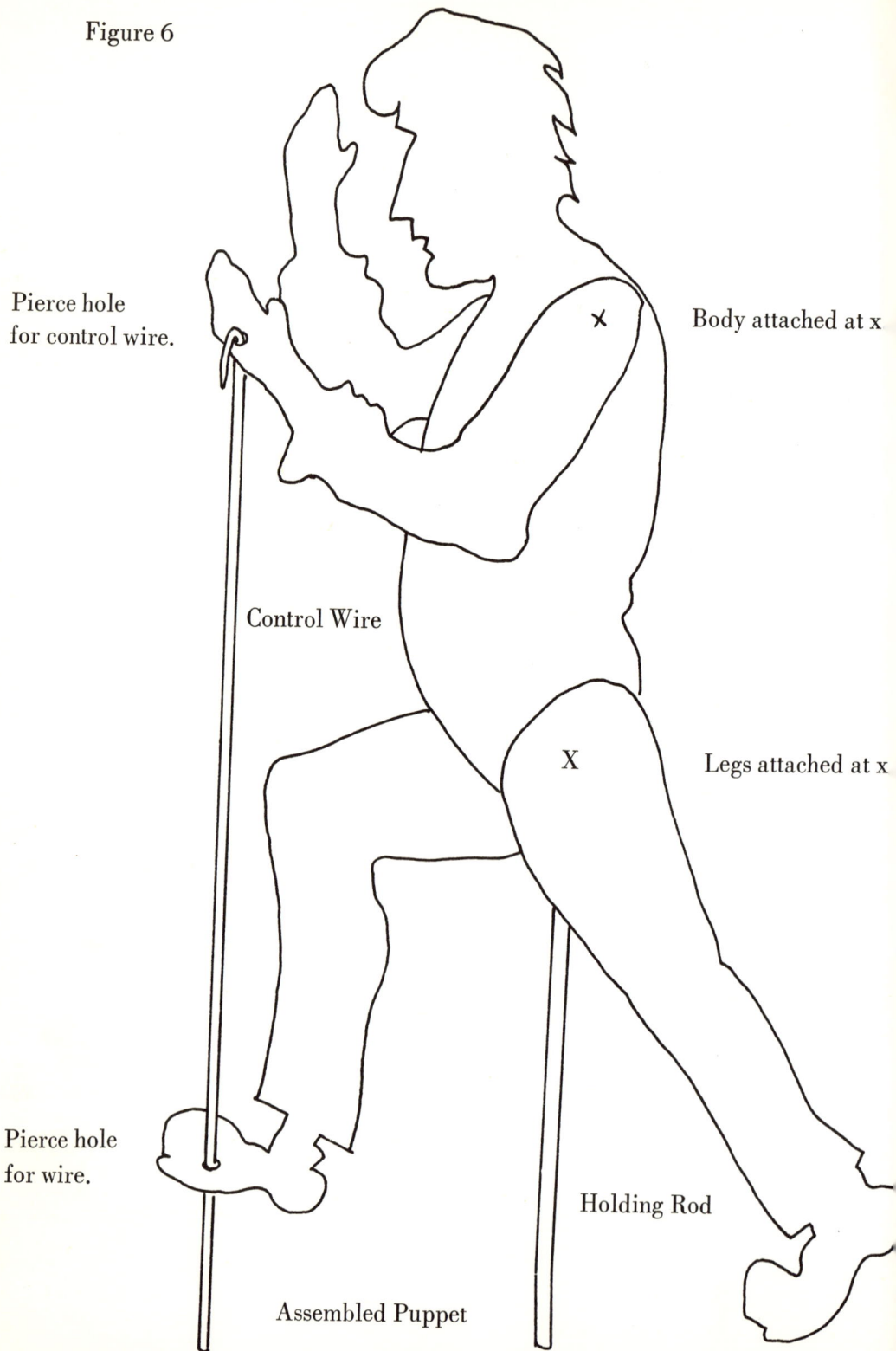

Figure 6

Pierce hole
for control wire.

Body attached at x

Control Wire

Legs attached at x

Pierce hole
for wire.

Holding Rod

Assembled Puppet

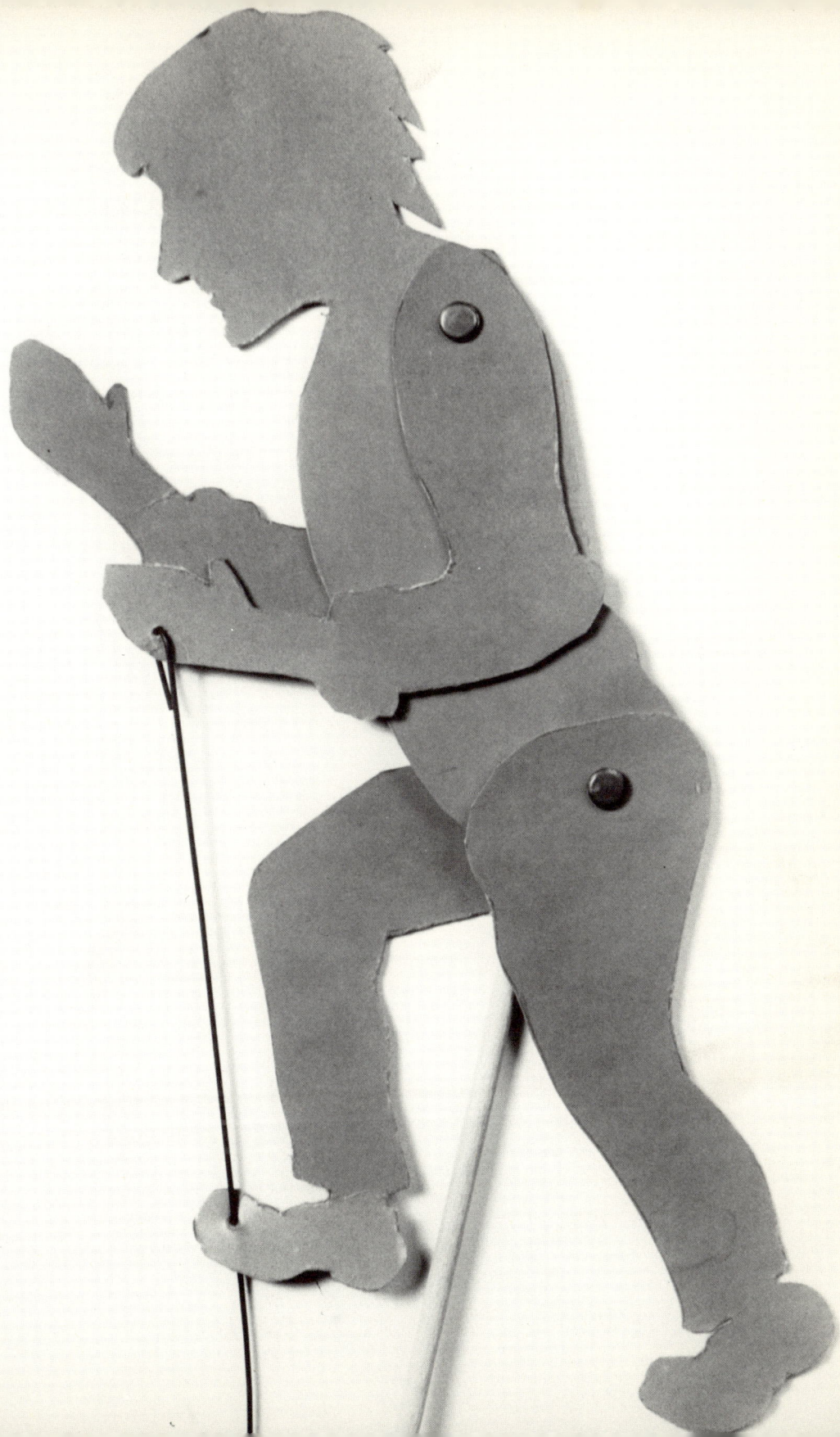

In the second act, when Lincoln wrestles with Armstrong in front of the store, simply have a backdrop with the exterior of the country store painted on it. A group of rod puppets can represent a crowd of people, including Armstrong's gang.

Action:

Armstrong and his gang are tough and have strong, arrogant voices. Lincoln is slow in speech as well as action. However, when he wrestles, he makes strong, quick movements.

ST. VALENTINE'S DAY

A Surprise for Mr. Winkle

HELEN REIN McKAY

Nancy lived on Blueberry Road. She lived next door to Mr. Winkle, the mailman.

There was a mailbox in front of every house on Blueberry Road. There was one at the front of Mr. Winkle's house too.

Mr. Winkle's mailbox was not the same as the rest. Every time Nancy saw it, she felt sad. Every other box on Blueberry Road was always silver-shiny, and its flag was a happy red. Mr. Winkle's mailbox was rusty and snow-covered, and its flag hung all the way down!

All winter Mr. Winkle walked up the road in his black boots and stopped at the shiny boxes. He opened their doors and let the sunshine in. Then he put in the mail.

He never stopped once at his own mailbox. Its door was never opened up to let the sunshine in. So the box just stood getting rustier and more snow-covered, with its flag drooping all the way down.

Poor Mr. Winkle! He brought letters to everyone else and never got one of his own. Nancy was sure she knew how he felt. She had wished for a long time that she could have a letter of her very own.

Sometimes a family letter came and someone wrote, "Tell

Nancy 'hello,' " or, "Give a hug to Nancy," but that wasn't
the least like reaching in the mailbox and pulling out a letter
of her very own.

Each day when she saw Mr. Winkle, Nancy put on her coat
and mittens and crunched through the snow to her gate. She
waited for Mr. Winkle to open her box.

Then she would ask excitedly, "Any letter for me?"

Mr. Winkle would hunt through his pack and say, "Looks
as if your letter didn't come today."

"Guess I'll never get my very own letter," Nancy sighed
one cold morning early in February.

Mr. Winkle said, "I never have a letter either."

Nancy watched him hurry past the rusty, snow-covered
mailbox at his front gate. Just then she had a great big thought.
It was a "February-the-fourteenth" kind of thought.

She hurried inside and found her scissors and a piece of
red paper. She took a long time to cut out a heart and write
the words. This is what she wrote on the heart:

Dear Mr. Winkle,

   I think your mailbox is rusty because it has never
been opened to hold a letter or to let the sunshine in.
So I am sending you a valentine. I hope it will make
you happy, and your mailbox happy, too.

   Love from your valentine friend.

Nancy went to town with Dad and pushed the valentine
through the mail slot in the big post office.

When next she saw Mr. Winkle, Nancy ran to the gate and
called as always, "Any letter for me?"

Mr. Winkle called back, "Looks as if your letter didn't come
today, but what do you think? I got a letter!" Mr. Winkle

grinned broadly and said, "I'm going to put it into my mailbox
so I can have the fun of taking it out when I get home. I wonder who was nice enough to write to me?"

Nancy pushed her hand against her mouth so her smile
wouldn't give her away.

The next day at the gate on Blueberry Road, Nancy asked
her same question.

This time Mr. Winkle didn't answer. He was busy looking
deep down in his mail pouch. At last he pulled out the whitest
and largest envelope Nancy had ever seen.

"You suppose this letter could be for you?" asked Mr.
Winkle, wrinkling his forehead. "It's addressed to a 'Valentine Friend of Mr. Winkle's on Blueberry Road.'"

"Well, I don't know—" said Nancy slowly.

Mr. Winkle looked worried. "No one else on Blueberry
Road will claim it. Might as well take it. It just might be for
you." He put it into her mailbox and closed the door.

Nancy was off the gate and by the mailbox in a wink. She
shivered with joy. She reached into the mailbox and pulled
out the envelope. At last she had a letter of her very own!

Inside the envelope was a red heart pasted on a white lacy
doily. This is what Nancy read:

Dear Friend!
    Thank you for your valentine. I was glad to have my
    door opened at last to let some sunshine in. Here is a
    valentine for you!
    Mr. Winkle's Mail Box

Mr. Winkle started to walk away. "Think I'll stop a minute
by that mailbox of mine."

Now Nancy turned toward Mr. Winkle's mailbox. Her eyes

blinked twice. There was Mr. Winkle's box all silver-shiny, with its flag standing straight and happy.

Nancy cried, "Why, it's the brightest box on Blueberry Road!"

"I think I'll open it every day to let the sunshine in," said Mr. Winkle. "Sometime I might be lucky enough to get another valentine or a letter."

"I know you will," said Nancy, "I'll—maybe you will get a letter every week."

"My," said Mr. Winkle. "That would be fine. A letter from a friend each week! I surely would have the shiniest box, the happiest box on all of Blueberry Road!"

Mailman Puppet

Materials:
brown felt
fabric, any color
black felt
four buttons
straight pins
needle and black thread, if costume is to be sewn
stapler and staples, if costume is to be stapled
scissors
ruler
tracing paper
Elmer' Glue-All
3-inch styrofoam ball
green felt
red knitting yarn

44

black knitting yarn
scraps of cardboard
scraps of black construction paper

Directions:

TROUSERS:

1. Measure and cut two pieces of fabric, 10 inches long, 6 inches wide. Loosely roll the 10 inch side of each. Flatten each roll and close the side opening with a needle and thread, or staple. These become trouser legs.

2. Sew or staple the two together at one end by overlapping one over the other in a slanted position (Figure 1). This will give you a more accurate shape for trousers.

BOOTS:

1. Trace Figure 2 (see Tracing Directions). Lay the pattern on the fold of a double piece of black felt. Pin it and cut it out.

2. Remove the pins and pattern. With a needle and doubled thread, sew around the opening of the boot.

3. Slip the boot over the bottom of the trouser leg. If it does not stay on, tack it to trouser.

4. Do the same with the second boot.

JACKET:

1. Trace Figure 3 and make a full-sized pattern from it.

2. Lay the full-sized pattern on two pieces of brown felt. Pin it in place. Cut out the felt. Remove the pins and pattern.

3. Pin the two pieces of felt together, except for the sleeve and bottom openings. Baste. Remove pins.

4. Sew around the basting with running stitches. Remove basting.

ATTACHING TROUSERS TO JACKET:

1. Slip the top of the trousers through the bottom of the jacket, up to the neckline.

45

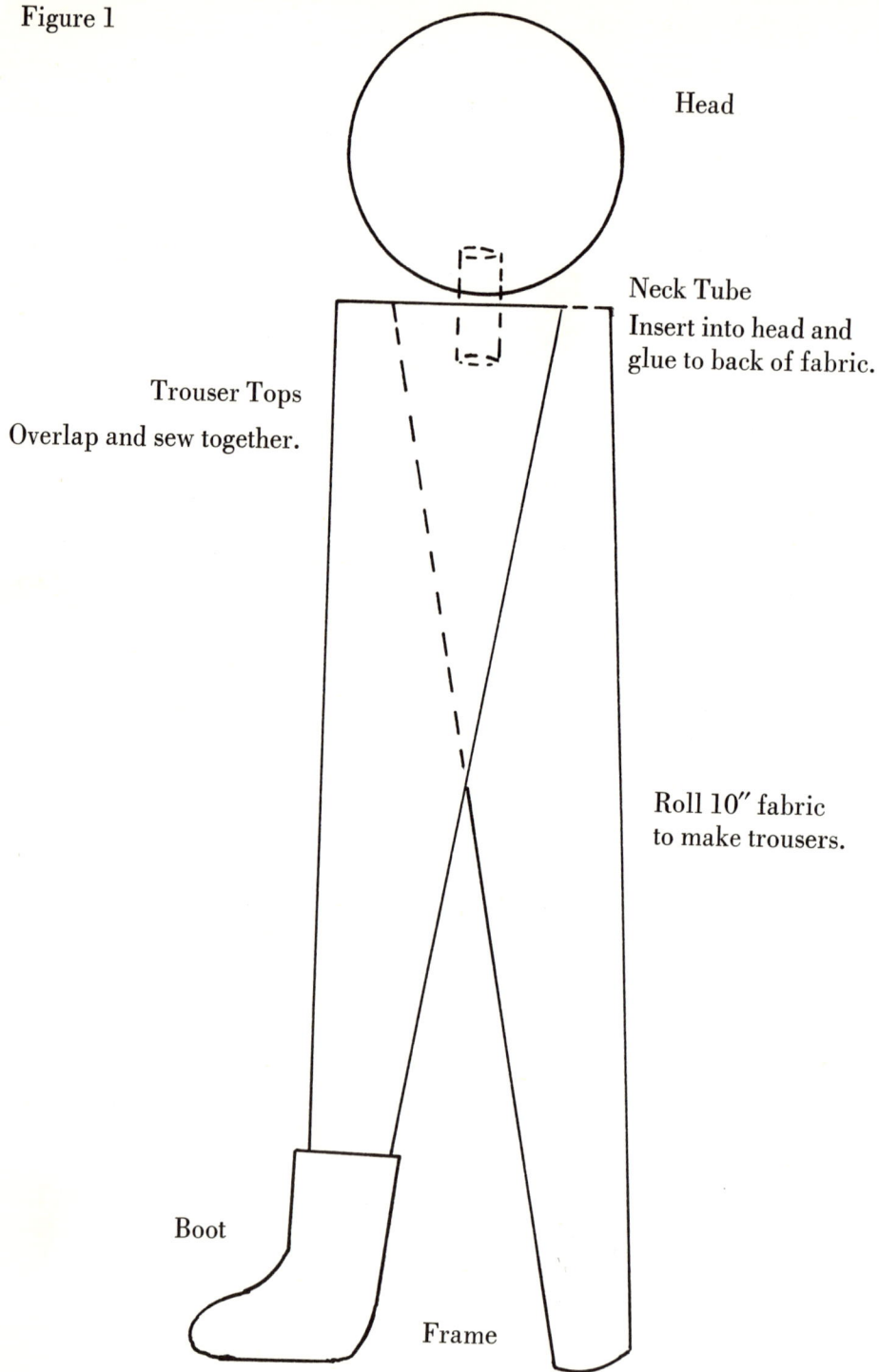

Figure 1

Head

Neck Tube
Insert into head and
glue to back of fabric.

Trouser Tops
Overlap and sew together.

Roll 10″ fabric
to make trousers.

Boot

Frame

Figure 2   On Fold

Boot
Trace and cut out.

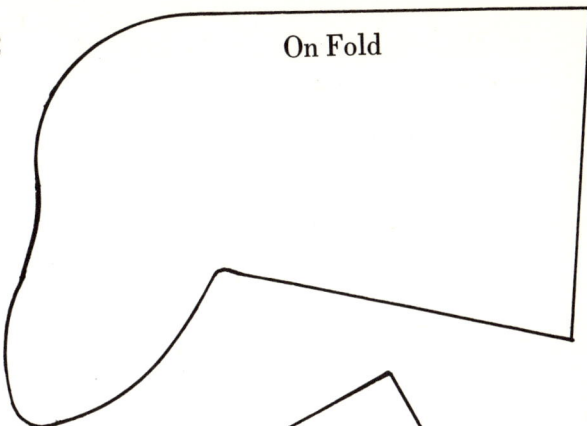

Figure 3

On Fold

Jacket
Trace and cut out.

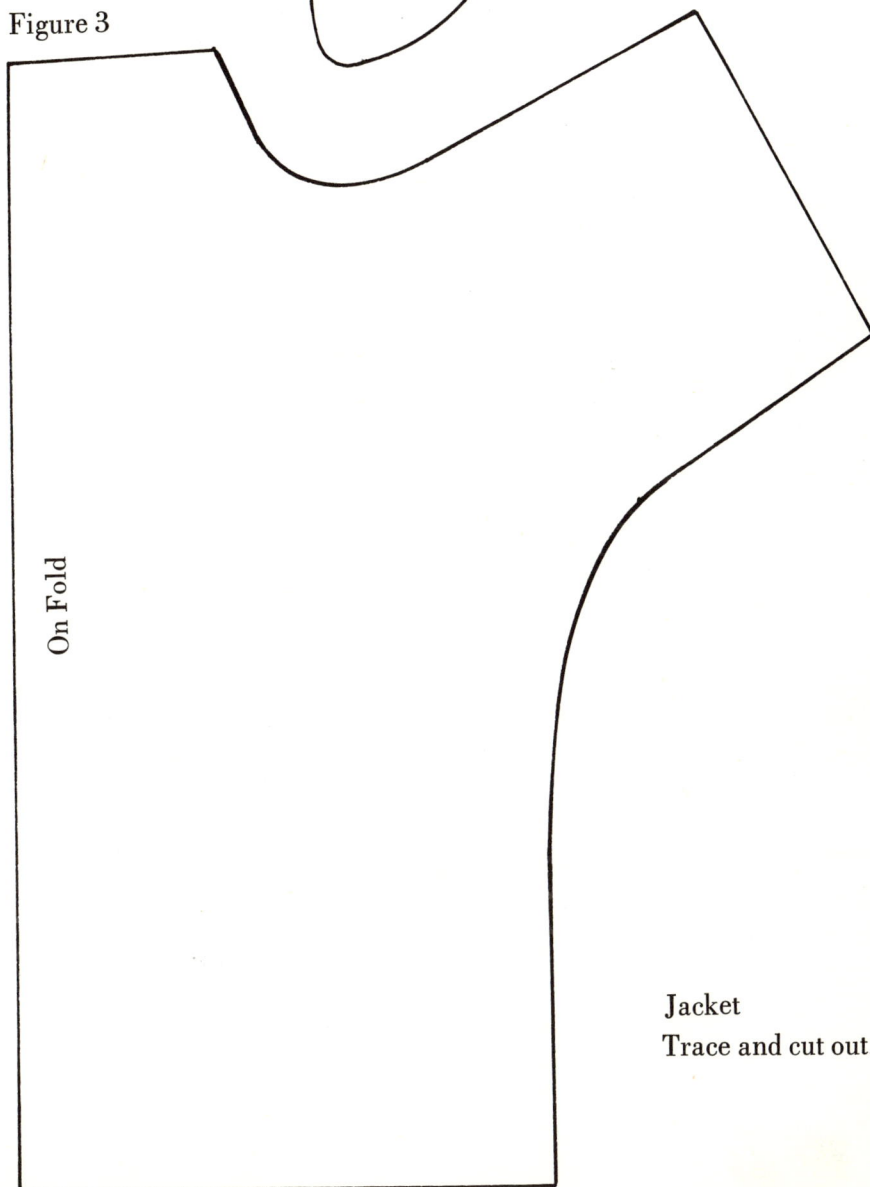

2. Pin the front of the jacket *only,* to the top of the trousers. Sew these together or staple them. This leaves the back part of the jacket open to slip your hand through.

COLLAR:

1. Trace Figure 4.

2. Lay the pattern on the fold of a doubled piece of brown felt. Pin them together. Cut around the pattern. Remove the pins and pattern.

3. Drape the collar around the jacket neckline. Pin the back of collar to back of neckline only. Pin the front of collar to front of jacket, with the trouser top attached to it. This will provide an opening for your index finger so that you can move the puppet's neck.

4. Sew down the top opening of the collar with running stitches.

5. Sew four small, evenly spaced buttons down the front of the jacket.

HEAD:

1. Make the neck from an empty toilet-paper tube. Open the tube and roll it around your index finger. Measure a 3 inch piece. Remove it from your finger while it is still rolled, cut off the excess, and glue the rolled tube securely. Apply glue to the outer surface of half the tube.

2. Cut a narrow strip of brown crepe paper and wind it around the cardboard tube. Dab glue at the end to hold.

3. Cut a hole at the base of a styrofoam ball making it large enough so that you can insert the neck tube into it. If possible, use a curved grapefruit knife.

4. Insert the neck tube into the hole, twisting it in place. Be sure it fits snugly. If not, dab glue at one end of the tube to hold.

5. Place the head over a dowel on a stand to facilitate working with it.

Figure 4

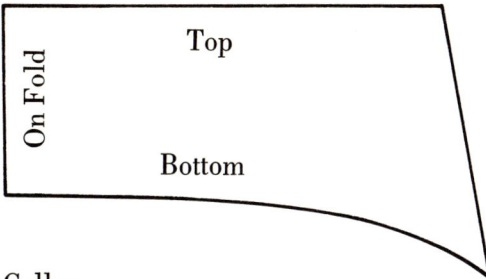

On Fold

Top

Bottom

Collar
Trace and cut out.

Figure 5

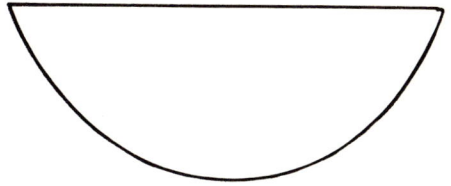

Visor
Trace and cut out.

HAT:

1. Cut a piece of green felt, $1\frac{1}{4}$ by $9\frac{1}{2}$ inches. Measure the diameter of the head for the exact size, and sew the ends of the felt together, overlapping one edge over the other.

2. Make a 3 inch diameter circle on a piece of cardboard (see Basic Shapes). Place the cardboard circle on a piece of green felt and trace it. Cut out the felt circle. Pin it to the band, and sew them together with an overhand stitch. The crown is now completed.

3. Trace Figure 5. Place the visor pattern on green felt, pin it, and cut it out. Remove pins and pattern. Pin the visor to the crown and sew them together with running stitches.

4. Dab glue to the inner front, back, and sides of the hat and position it on the head. Press it to hold and let it dry.

EARMUFFS:

1. Make a cardboard circle, about $1\frac{1}{4}$ inches in diameter. Apply glue on one side. Starting in the center, wind red knitting yarn in a spiral until the circle is covered. Cut off excess yarn. Press the yarn against the cardboard base and let it dry.

2. Repeat Step 1 to make the second earmuff.

3. Apply glue on the back of each earmuff and position one on each side of the mailman's head. Press to hold and allow to dry. Insert a straight pin in the center of each earmuff and through the styrofoam.

49

FEATURES:

1. To make the mailman's eyes, trace Figure 19 on page 88. Cut two from black construction paper. Apply glue to the back of each and position on the face.

2. Cut a small circle for the nose from black construction paper. Glue it to the face.

3. To add a mustache, apply a little glue under the nose. Cut several very small pieces of black knitting yarn, and apply each piece over the glue, straight up and down, with a tweezer if possible. Press to hold. Allow to dry. You may make your own style mustache with yarn or draw it on with black ink.

4. Attach the head to the body. Apply glue around the neck tube. With one hand, open the neckline of the costume and carefully insert the glue-covered tube into it. Press the front and back of the costume against tube to hold. Allow to dry.

MAIL POUCH:

1. Cut two pieces of felt of any color, about 4 by $2\frac{1}{2}$ inches.

2. Sew the sides and bottom together, leaving the top open.

3. Cut a strip of felt of the same color, about $\frac{1}{2}$ inch by 9 inches.

4. Sew or staple one end to the front and the other to the back, just inside the pouch opening.

5. With flair pen or black India ink, letter U. S. MAIL on the front and back of the pouch.

6. Fill pouch with make-believe mail and a heart-shaped valentine.

7. Hang the pouch over the mailman's shoulder.

Suggestions for Other Puppet:

1. The little girl is made the same way as the mailman except that she is smaller and wears a different-colored costume. She also wears a woolen scarf wrapped around her head and neck.

Insert middle finger
into one arm.

Insert the index finger
into the head.

Insert thumb
into one arm.

Figure 6

Holding Hand Puppet
for Action

Insert hand
into costume.

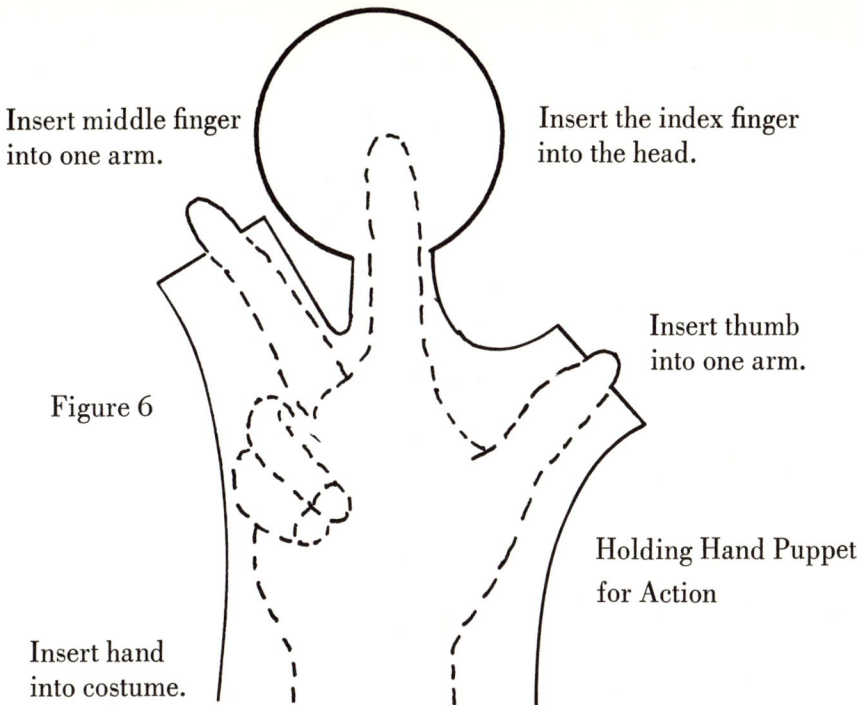

2. Both puppets may have papier-maché heads instead of styrofoam.

Holding the Puppet for Action:

1. Place your hand inside the jacket, behind the waist.

2. Place your index finger into the neck tube and inside the head.

3. Put your thumb and middle finger through the mailman's sleeves. See Figure 6.

4. Move your thumb and middle finger to make the puppet's arms move. Use your index finger to move its head forward, backward, or sideways. Bend your wrist to make the puppet bow and walk.

5. Practice your motions, looking at the puppet or watching it in a mirror to see how the movements will look to the audience.

51

Production Notes

Technique:

The narrator reads the story while the actors perform. The narrator stands either beside the stage or behind it. The action and the narration should be carefully synchronized.

Cast:

Mr. Winkle, the mailman
Nancy, a little girl
narrator

Scenery and Properties:

A winter outdoor scene is painted on the backdrop. Two or three snow-covered mailboxes on posts are attached to the floor of the stage. Each has a name and a flag on it. These are constructed of cardboard. The mailboxes, except Mr. Winkle's, are covered with aluminum foil. The flags are covered with red construction paper. Mr. Winkle's mailbox is covered with brown construction paper. His mailbox is dilapidated, its flag drooping, and appears to be falling off the post. It is loosely attached to the floor with Scotch tape. Bare trees laden with snow are securely fixed to the floor. White absorbent cotton is used for snow. There is an open door at the back of the stage through which Nancy enters and exits. In front of the door is a gate, which Nancy hangs over to greet Mr. Winkle, and beside the gate is her mailbox. The mail pouch contains small letters and Nancy's valentine.

Action:

The action takes place outdoors in a clearing surrounded by snow-covered trees. There is a row of mailboxes. The puppets pantomime. Mr. Winkle walks up the road, stops at the mailboxes, and puts mail in. Nancy is anxious to receive mail of

53

her own. Therefore, when she sees the mailman, her voice is excited. When there is no mail, she is disappointed. When Nancy hurries inside to write her valentine for the mailman, and then goes to town with her Dad to mail it, she is simply absent from the stage while the narrator tells the audience what she is doing.

There is an interim between the time Mr. Winkle receives his valentine on one day and the time that Nancy receives hers on the next. To show this Nancy and Mr. Winkle exit, and re-enter the stage after a short lapse of time. During this time, Mr. Winkle's mailbox is taken off the stage and a shiny new one is quickly substituted. Props are often changed in front of the audience by Chinese and Japanese puppeteers and by some of our modern puppet men.

When Mr. Winkle looks for Nancy's mail, he slips the mail pouch off his shoulder and puts it on the floor. He looks through it slowly for a while, adding to Nancy's suspense, before he pulls out a valentine for her.

WASHINGTON'S BIRTHDAY

Washington and the First Flight in America

LAURA ROSS

Characters:
George Washington
Monsieur Blanchard
stranger
spectators

Properties:
inflated balloon
small letter
trees
rifle
desk
chair
American flag (small)
French flag (small)

55

Act I

Narrator (*from behind closed curtain*): In the years when Americans were founding the Republic, other exciting things were happening in the world. In France, two brothers made history with their first successful flight. They were lifted and carried into the air in a balloon. In America, many attempts were made in the following ten years, but none were successful. It was not until French balloonist Monsieur Jean Blanchard went to Philadelphia, when George Washington was President, that the first air voyage was made in America.

At Curtain Rise:

A crowd of people stand in a public square. In a central clearing is an inflated balloon, and close to it stands M. Blanchard, making a last-minute inspection. He checks the cords of the balloon and peers into the basket. The spectators move about animatedly with an air of great excitement. Strains of band music play a lively tune in the background.

Spectators (*excited*): He's coming! He's coming! Here comes President Washington!

Washington (*enters with a letter in his hand as the band music continues to play. When it stops, Blanchard approaches the President and doffs his hat. They shake hands*): Monsieur Blanchard, my good friend Benjamin Franklin has informed me of the success of the balloon flight in France. Now your knowledge and daring are bringing to us the first balloon flight in America. May you succeed in your endeavor and return to our city, where I shall anxiously wait to hear your account. (The President hands Blanchard a piece of paper.) I hope you will not need this letter, but in the event that you do, don't hesitate to use it.

Blanchard (*takes the letter from Washington, reads it, then folds it and puts it in his pocket. He bows to Washington*):

56

Thank you, Mr. President, for your good wishes and for the letter. (*He leaps into the basket. A murmur of admiration rises from the spectators as the balloon lifts up and disappears. Strains of band music are heard again as the curtain closes.*)

Act II

At Curtain Rise:

A clearing in a wooded area. Monsieur Blanchard lands and hops out of the basket. He hears a sound behind the trees, looks around, and sees a stranger watching him from the shelter of the trees and aiming a rifle at him. The stranger comes forward, still pointing his rifle at Blanchard.

Blanchard (*surprised and excited*): No, no, Monsieur! Do not shoot! Do not shoot!

Stranger (*still pointing rifle*): Don't move, or I *will* shoot. What business do you have here? And what is that fangdangle monster you have there?

Blanchard (*very excited*): Please, Monsieur! First put that rifle down, and then I will tell you!

Stranger (*still pointing rifle at Blanchard*): Nothing of the sort. First you tell me. Then perhaps I'll put the rifle down.

Blanchard (*pleading*): Please, Monsieur, do not shoot. Washington knows. Yes, President Washington knows. Here, see, he gave me this letter to show you.

Stranger (*looks at the letter; then shakes his head*): Can't read. What does it say?

Blanchard: If I read it to you will you believe it?

Stranger: Can't say I will. How do I know you're not a spy?

Blanchard (*showing the letter to the stranger once more*): Here. See the seal? It is the red government seal of George Washington!

Stranger (*looks at the seal, then lowers his rifle*): Why didn't you say so in the first place! What does it say?

Blanchard (*reading from the letter*): It says: "George Washington, President of the United States of America: To All to Whom These Presents Shall Come. The bearer hereof, Mr. Blanchard, a citizen of France, proposing to ascend in a balloon from the city of Philadelphia, at 10 o'clock A.M. this day, to pass in such direction and to descend in such place as circumstances may render most convenient. These are therefore to recommend to all citizens of the United States, and others, that in his passage, descent, return, or journeying elsewhere, they oppose no hindrance or molestation to the said Mr. Blanchard; And that on the contrary, they receive and aid him with that humanity and good will, which may render honour to their country, and justice to an individual so distinguished by his efforts to establish and advance an art, in order to make it useful to mankind in general.

Seal: Given under my hand and seal, at the city of Philadelphia, this ninth day of January, one thousand seven hundred and ninety three, Signed: George Washington"

Stranger: The name George Washington is dearer to us than any other in this land. We respect him as we do our own father. Come with me and welcome to my humble house. Stay as long as you wish and make yourself at home with us. (*Blanchard and the stranger exit arm in arm and the curtain closes.*)

Act III

At Curtain Rise:

A room in George Washington's headquarters. The President is seated at his desk, thinking. In a short while Monsieur Blanchard enters, carrying the tricolors of France. Washington rises to greet him. Both shake hands.

58

Washington: Welcome back Monsieur Blanchard. I am most happy to see that you have returned safely.

Blanchard: Thank you Mr. President. My balloon journey was successful, but I almost did not return.

Washington (*amazed*): Almost did not return? I could think only of your journey and your safe return.

Blanchard: Mr. President, nothing would have kept me from returning to report to you of my successful landing in New Jersey, except that I was almost shot by a farmer. He thought I was a spy and my balloon, a monster from the sky. If it were not for your passport of good will, I would not have returned. For this, I thank you, Mr. President. Accept in exchange the French flag, which like yours, stands for freedom and unity. (*Blanchard hands over the tricolors of France to Washington, who accepts it willingly. They shake hands and the curtain closes to strains of music in the background*).

Washington Puppet

Materials:
Bristol board, white
railroad board, colored
construction paper, black
pipe cleaner, red
felt or cloth, any color
two fancy buttons
needle and thread or stapler and staples
scissors
Elmer's Glue-All
ruler
pencil

59

tracing paper
yarn, or gift tie, any color
strip of narrow ribbon, any color
straight pins

Directions:

HEAD:

1. Measure and cut a strip of Bristol board, 6 by $2\frac{1}{2}$ inches, for the head, and construct a cylinder (see Basic Shapes). This cylinder will be $2\frac{1}{2}$ inches long.

2. Make the neck with a $3\frac{1}{2}$ by $2\frac{1}{4}$ inch strip. This cylinder will be $2\frac{1}{4}$ inches long.

3. Apply glue $\frac{1}{2}$ inch from the edge of one end of the neck cylinder.

4. Insert this end about $\frac{1}{2}$ inch into the bottom of the head cylinder. Press the glued portion against the back of the head cylinder. Hold it until it dries. See Figure 1.

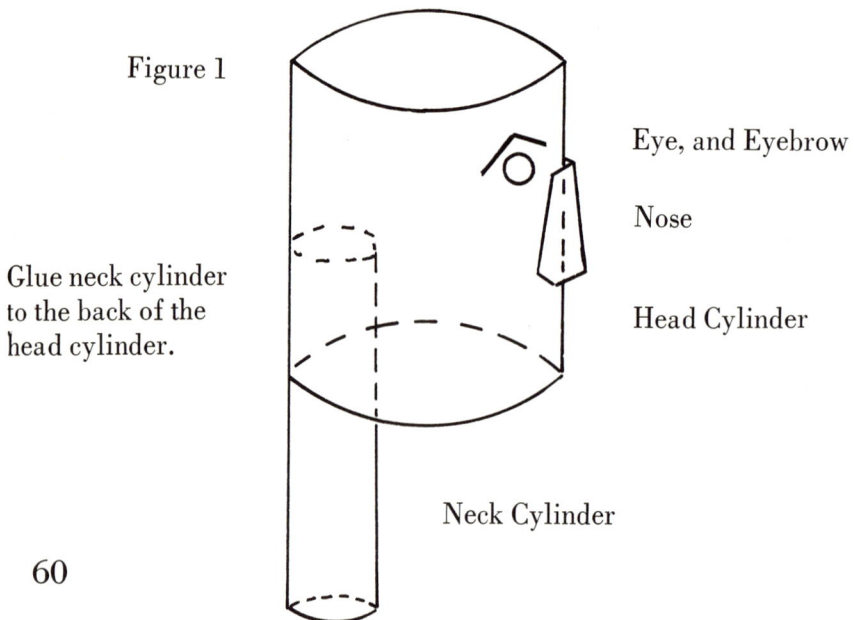

Figure 1

Eye, and Eyebrow

Nose

Glue neck cylinder
to the back of the
head cylinder.

Head Cylinder

Neck Cylinder

60

Side View of Head and Neck

5. To make hair, cut about ten 5 inch long strands of knitting yarn or yarn gift-tie. Apply glue to one end of each strand and insert it about $\frac{1}{2}$ inch into the top opening of the cylinder at the back of the head. Glue the pieces side by side, bending each one over the edge and down against the back of the cylinder. Strips of crepe paper can be used instead of yarn.

6. When all strands have been attached to the head, secure them by pressing each to the back of the cylinder with an additional dab of glue. Allow to dry.

7. Pull the hair back and gather the loose strands together with a narrow ribbon tied into a bow.

HAT:

1. Trace Figure 2 to make a pattern (see Tracing Directions). Cut out two pieces, front and back, from colored railroad board.

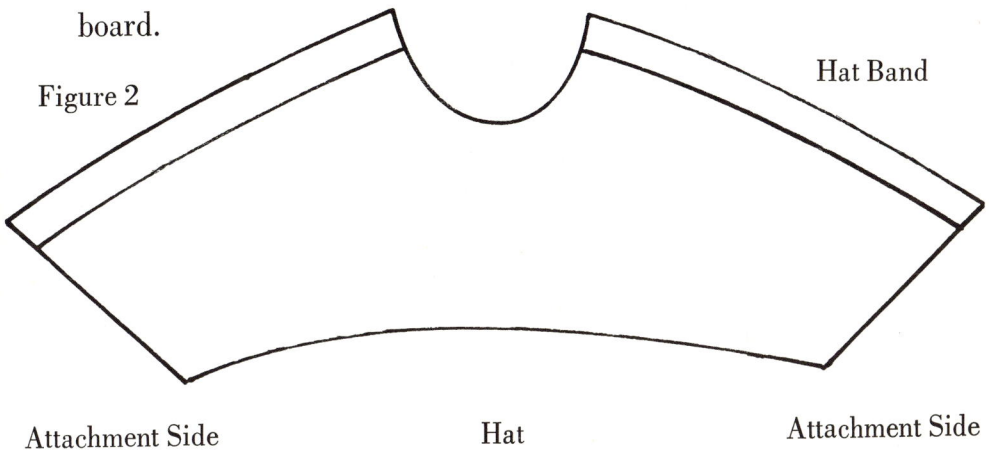

Figure 2

Hat Band

Attachment Side   Hat   Attachment Side

Trace and cut out.

2. Cut a strip of black construction paper, about 12 inches long and $\frac{1}{4}$ inch wide, and glue it across the front and back top edges. Cut a curved strip to fit the curve and glue it on.

61

3. Glue the front and back together at each side. Press to hold. Allow to dry.

4. Dab glue to the bottom inner edges of the front and back of the hat. Slip it over the head cylinder, about ½ inch from the top of the head. Press to hold and allow to dry.

FACIAL FEATURES:

1. To make the nose, trace Figure 3 and transfer it to black construction paper.

Figure 3

Nose

Trace and cut out.

Fold on dotted lines.

2. Apply glue to both side tabs and position the nose on the front of the head cylinder. Press to hold. Allow to dry.

3. For eyes, cut two small circles from black construction paper. Glue them on. Press to hold and allow to dry.

4. Draw eyebrows over the eyes with black ink.

5. Shape a mouth from a small piece of red pipe cleaner. Glue it under the nose, as illustrated in the photograph. Hold it in place and let it dry.

COSTUME:

1. Trace Figure 4 to make a pattern.

2. Using a 6 by 11½ inch piece of felt, fold the longer side in half so that it is 6 inches wide and 5¾ inches long. The fold at the top will go over the shoulders. Fold the felt once more, lengthwise, so that it is 3 inches wide and 5¾ inches long.

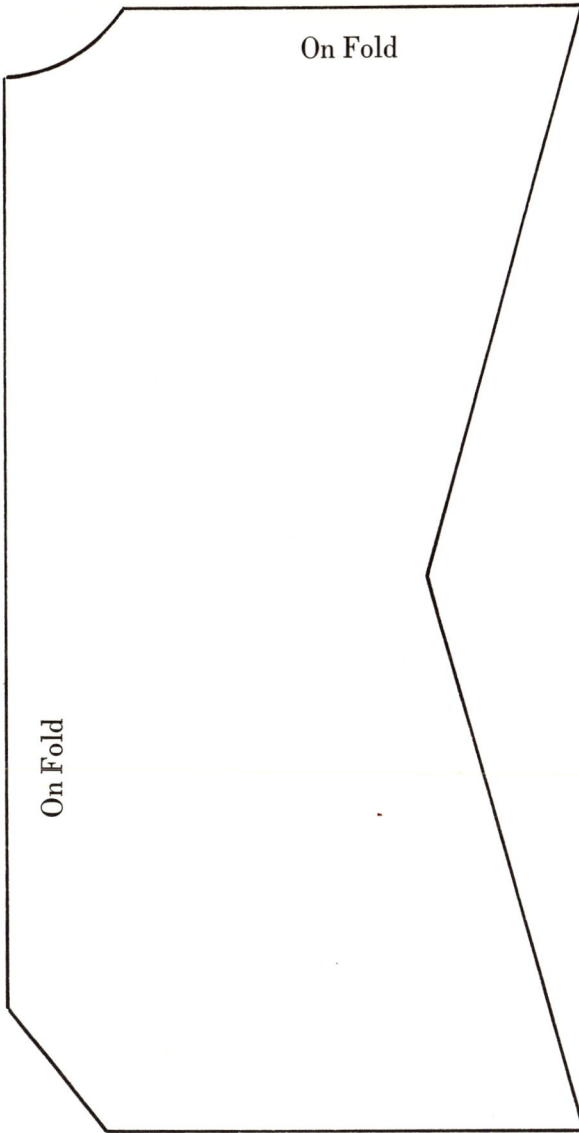

On Fold

Figure 4

Jacket

Trace and cut out.

On Fold

3. Pin the paper pattern to the felt, placing it on the folds, as noted. Cut around the pattern, but do not cut the folded segments of felt. Remove pins and pattern.

63

4. Make two side straps, each 1½ inches by ½ inch. Sew or staple the ends of each strap to the sides of the jacket, connecting the front and back, as illustrated in Figure 5.

5. Trim the jacket by sewing rickrack or narrow ribbon down the front, as shown in Figure 5.

6. Sew buttons to the front of the jacket.

7. For a neck ruffle, gather small piece of lace or discarded handkerchief. Sew or staple it to the front of the jacket neck opening.

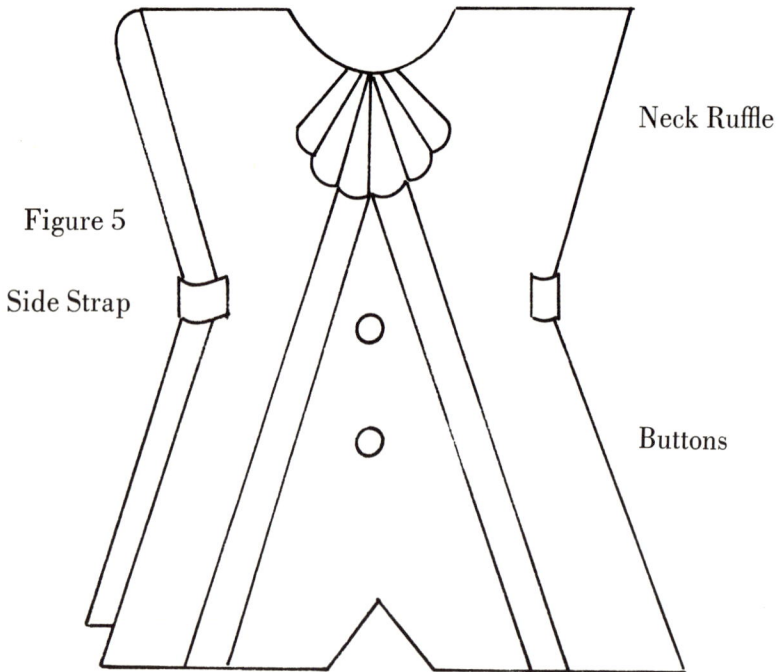

Neck Ruffle

Figure 5

Side Strap

Buttons

Assembled Jacket

ATTACHING HEAD TO COSTUME:

1. Apply glue around the neck cylinder just under the head.

2. Insert the neck cylinder into the jacket neck opening as far down as necessary, allowing only the head to show above it. Press the front and back of the jacket against the glued neck cylinder. Allow to dry.

3. The George Washington hand puppet is now complete.

Suggestions for Other Puppets in the Play:
Make M. Blanchard the same as George Washington, using hair of a different color and adding a small pocket to the costume to distinguish one puppet from the other. The stranger may be constructed with cylinders and operated like a hand puppet. He should carry a rifle, which can be cut out of cardboard. Silhouette stick puppets can be moved about in the background. Color them with crayon if you like.

Holding the Puppet for Action:
1. Place your hand inside the jacket, behind the waist.
2. Place your index finger through the neck cylinder and inside the head.
3. Insert your thumb and middle finger through the sleeves.
4. Your thumb and middle finger will serve as the puppet's arms. Move them to make the puppet's arms move. Use your index finger to move the head. Bend your wrist to make the puppet bow and walk.
5. Practice these motions.

Production Notes

Scenery and Properties:
On the backdrop is a scene of the village square with buildings painted on it. Spectators are also painted on the backdrop.

The most spectacular thing in this play is the balloon, an ordinary balloon, inflated with helium, if possible, to keep it aloft. Tie the opening with a string that is long enough to

control the balloon from below stage. If helium is not available, blow up the balloon, tie the opening with a short string, then tie the string to a thin rod so that the balloon can be pushed up and down from below stage. There is also a small gondola-like basket made of cardboard. This can be a tomato basket from the grocery store. You may, however, want to construct your own. Decorate it with small stars. Make a hole at each of the four corners of the cardboard basket. Tie a piece of string about 14 inches long through each hole. Attach the opposite end of each string to the top of the balloon with a small piece of masking tape. Staple or tape two small flags to each end of the gondola, the American Stars and Stripes and the tricolors of France, blue, white, and red. You may make your own flags by coloring small pieces of white construction paper and gluing each to a toothpick. See Figure 6.

In the second act trees are painted on the backdrop. There are also trees made of colored cardboard and secured to the floor of the stage.

In the third act, the stage is furnished with a desk and chair. The American flag is on the backdrop.

Action:

In the first act, there is an air of great excitement, shown by moving the stick puppets in the background.

When M. Blanchard enters the balloon basket, he is simply placed in it with his costume folded under him and his head showing above the basket. A puppeteer below stage, preferably the one holding Blanchard, holds the balloon down with the string or rod. Then he lets it go up just before the curtain closes at the end of the first act.

67

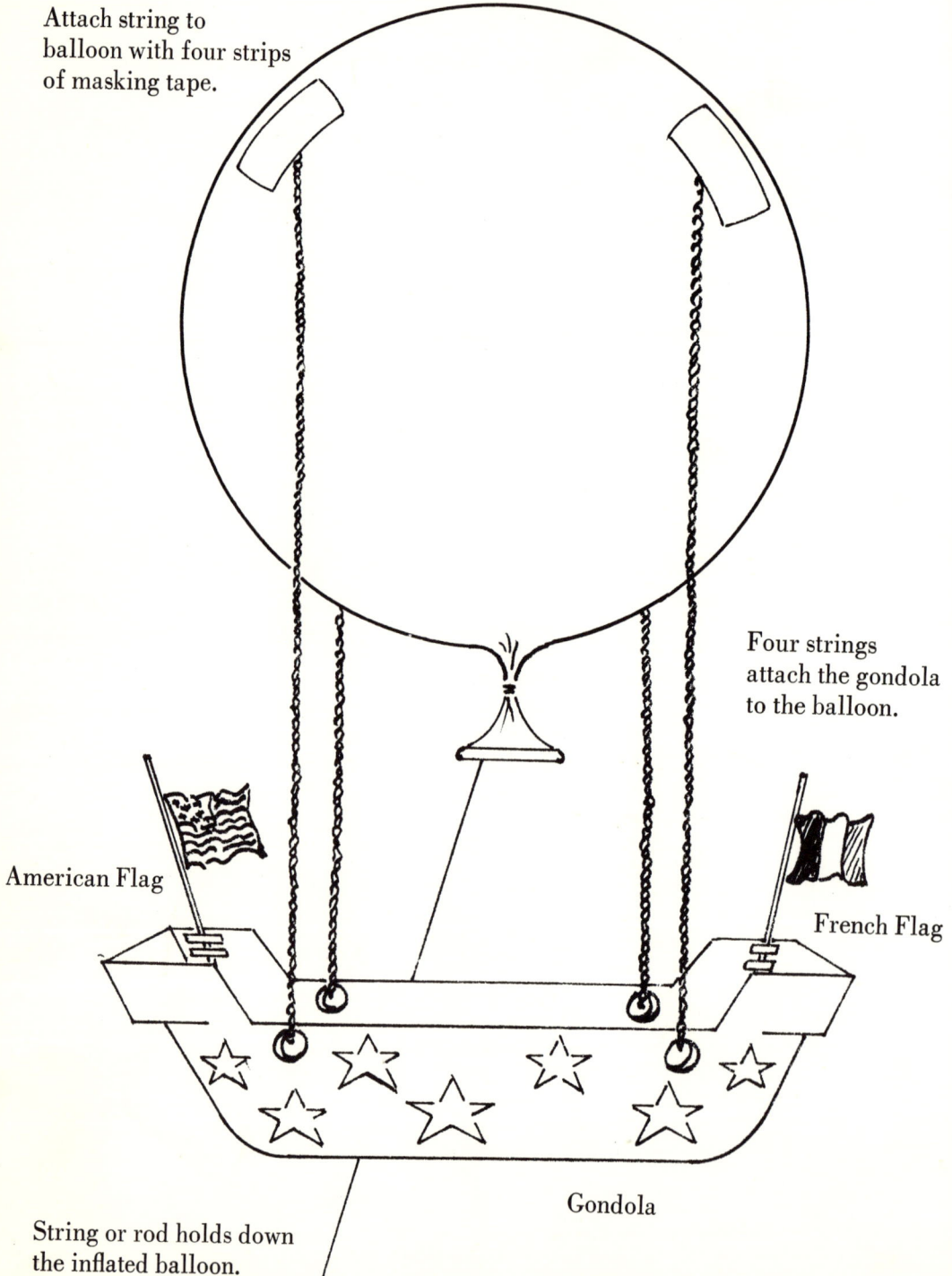

Figure 6

Inflated Balloon

Attach string to balloon with four strips of masking tape.

Four strings attach the gondola to the balloon.

American Flag

French Flag

Gondola

String or rod holds down the inflated balloon.

The action of the story builds up in the second act as the stranger threatens to shoot M. Blanchard as a spy. Blanchard is fearful for his life, and the stranger is determined to shoot him. The players express these feelings with their actions and voices. It is only when Blanchard reads Washington's letter aloud that the stranger puts his gun down.

ST. PATRICK'S DAY

The Lazy Leprechaun

JILL TAYLOR

In the country of Ireland, far over the sea, there once lived a lazy leprechaun named Liam.

Now leprechauns (who are really fairy shoemakers) are usually very hard workers. All night long, they busily sew and hammer shoes, and when dawn comes they leave them on the doorstep of anyone who has been especially kind to them.

Well, as you can imagine, the hardworking leprechauns didn't know what to do about Liam, the lazy leprechaun! While they were all stitching and hammering shoes, Liam just lay on his back in the tall grass, wiggled his toes in the air, and whistled or sang a pretty tune.

Sometimes he hummed a slow, lazy song—his toes barely moving at all. Sometimes he whistled an Irish jig—his toes fairly twinkling as they kept time to his music. But he never worked!

"He's a disgrace to the leprechaun tribe!" grumbled the other leprechauns. "Let's send him to live with the gnomes and goblins!" But one night, before they could send Liam away, a very important visitor came to the forest. It was the King of Ireland!

Reprinted from Instructor © March 1971, The Instructor Publications, Inc. Used by permission.

First his herald blew a loud blast on a trumpet and asked the leprechauns to gather in the bright moonlight.

After another trumpet fanfare, the King started speaking. "My friends, I need your help! My daughter, the Princess, will be married in seven days and we are planning the greatest celebration Ireland has ever known! I want all my subjects to have new shoes for the wedding—leprechaun shoes—so they can dance all night and never get tired. Will you make them for me?"

"Yes! Yes! Yes!" cried the leprechauns in their high shrill voices.

"Very good!" said the King. "If you succeed, I'll give each leprechaun a purse of gold!" And then the King went away.

Well, you never saw such activity in all your life! The leprechauns seized their hammers and needles and began to pound and stitch, until the woods rang with noise. All but Liam, the lazy leprechaun. He just lay in the tall grass; sang songs to himself; and wiggled his toes in the breeze.

For the first six days and nights the leprechauns kept hard at their task, but one by one they grew tired, until finally they had hardly enough strength left to lift a hammer to pound or to pick up a needle to sew—all but Liam.

Suddenly Liam stopped singing and listened very hard. "That's strange," he said to himself. The forest was absolutely silent! Slowly he sat up, looked around, and saw an amazing sight. The leprechauns had fallen sound asleep over the shoes they were making.

"Oh, dear!" exclaimed Liam. "This is terrible! The shoes will never be ready for the wedding!"

He jumped up and ran among the sleeping leprechauns, shaking them and trying to wake them up. But they were just too tired and kept right on sleeping!

71

Then Liam had an idea! Quickly he climbed into the nearest tree, sat on a limb right above the sleeping leprechauns, and began singing as loudly as he could. As he sang, he clapped his hands in time to the music.

> Hammer! Hammer! Stitch and sew!
> Wake up, leprechauns! Let's go!

Louder and faster he sang, harder and harder he clapped, until one by one each leprechaun lifted his head, staggered to his feet, and started hammering and sewing again. The music was so lively that their fingers moved swiftly and their hammers rose and fell quickly. When dawn came, the shoes were all finished.

Just in time, too. For in the distance, the leprechauns heard the sound of a trumpet and knew the King was coming.

The King was very joyful when he saw the huge pile of shoes the leprechauns had made. He gave each leprechaun a purse of gold, just as he had promised, and invited them to attend the wedding.

So the night of the Princess's wedding, the happy leprechauns made merry in the moonlight and danced every dance.

As for Liam, the lazy leprechaun—he just lay on his back in the grass, wiggled his toes in the breeze, and sang a happy wedding tune.

Leprechaun Marionette

A marionette is a puppet with strings attached to it. Sometimes it is called a "string puppet." The strings are manipulated from above the stage to make the puppet move.

In the "Lazy Leprechaun," one leprechaun dances a jig and

wiggles his toes. The others hammer and sew to make shoes. This kind of action is shown best with string puppets.

The marionette should have loosely constructed joints and a light costume to enable it to move smoothly and look as lifelike as possible.

Marionettes can be made in different ways with different materials. They can have many strings attached to their joints to give them a variety of movements or they can be made with fewer strings for simple basic movements, like the one in this book.

If you cannot sew, iron, drill, or saw, ask someone who knows how to help you. If a drill is not available, use a hammer and a thick nail to make holes in the control bar.

Follow each step carefully and you will see how easy it can be to make a marionette.

Making the Body

Materials:

1 inch thick soft wood, 3 by $1\frac{1}{2}$ inches, for chest
1 inch thick soft wood, $1\frac{1}{2}$ by $1\frac{1}{2}$ inches, for trunk
two $\frac{1}{2}$ inch diameter dowels, $2\frac{1}{2}$ inches long, for calves
two $\frac{1}{2}$ inch diameter dowels, 1 inch long, for thighs
two $\frac{1}{2}$ inch diameter dowels, 1 inch long, for arms
unbleached muslin, $\frac{1}{4}$ yard, or part of an old shirt or handkerchief
3 inch styrofoam ball, for head
stapler and staples, or several small nails and a hammer
one small screw eye
thin but sturdy wire, about $5\frac{1}{2}$ inches long for head attachment
scraps of black construction paper and green felt
black knitting yarn

73

scissors
tracing paper
pencil
ruler
Elmer's Glue-All

Directions:

CHEST:

1. Using the 3½ by 1½ inch block of wood, make a mark ½ inch from the right and left corners of the lower 3½ inch side. Draw a straight line from the upper-right corner to the lower-right mark (Figure 2). Do the same on the left side.
2. Saw along the penciled lines on both sides. The chest block should look like Figure 3.

Figure 2   Figure 3

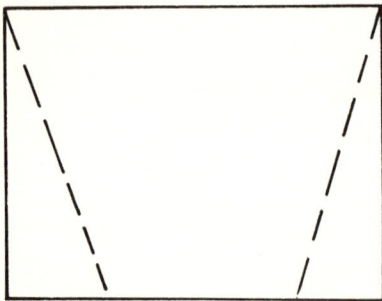

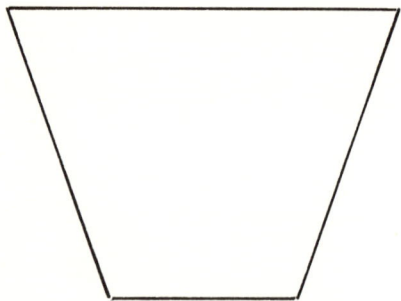

Uncut Chest Block   Cut Chest Block

3. Screw a screw eye into the center of the longer (top) side of the chest block.

74

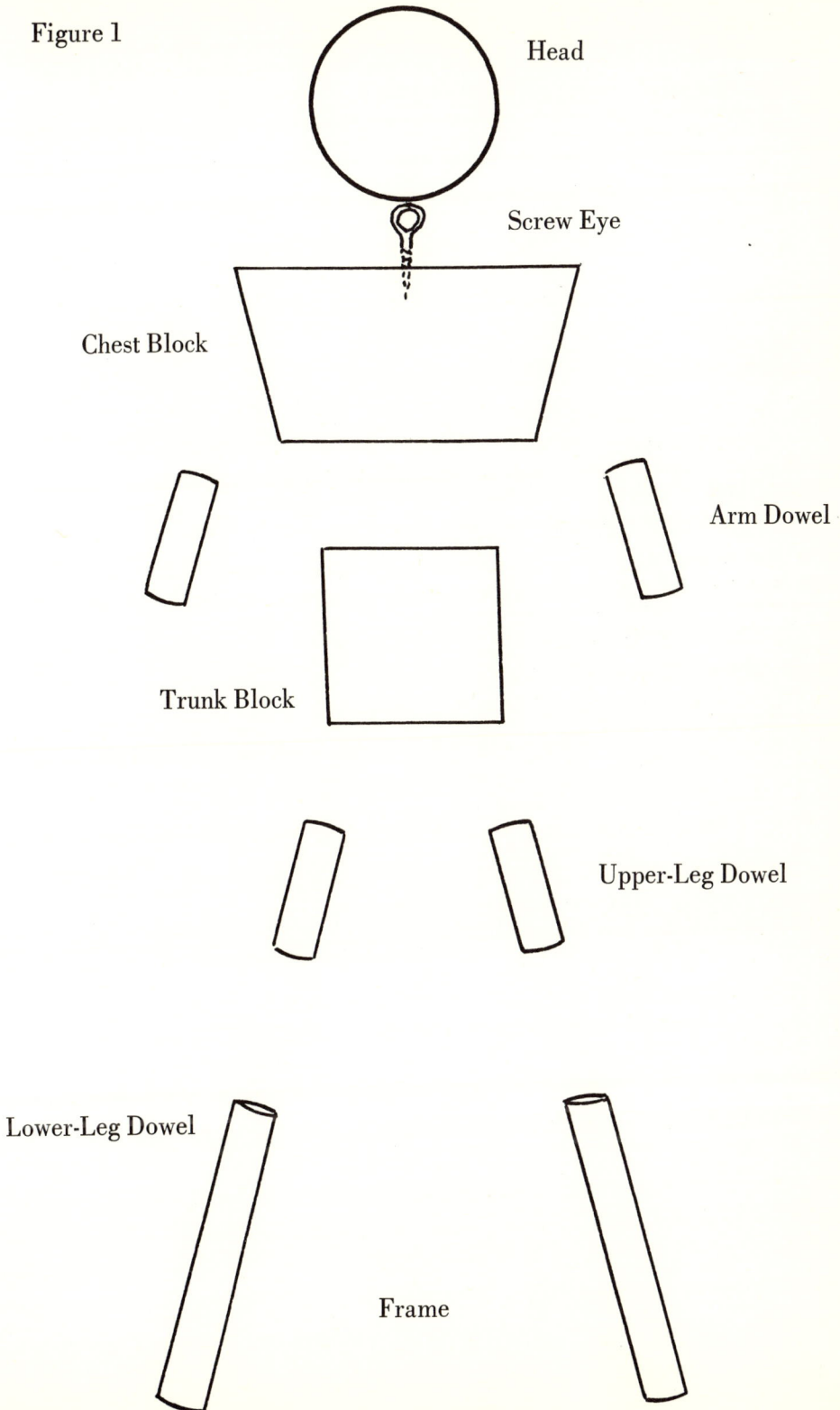

Figure 1

Head

Screw Eye

Chest Block

Arm Dowel

Trunk Block

Upper-Leg Dowel

Lower-Leg Dowel

Frame

TRUNK:

1. Use the $1\frac{1}{2}$ by $1\frac{1}{2}$ inch block of wood as it is. To attach it to the chest, cut a piece of muslin, 8 inches wide by $\frac{3}{4}$ inches long.

2. Wrap one 8 inch side of the muslin around the bottom of the chest block, about $\frac{1}{2}$ inch from edge. Overlap excess muslin.

3. Glue, staple, or nail the muslin securely to the wood on the front and back of chest.

4. Wrap the opposite 8 inch side of muslin around the top of the trunk block, about $\frac{1}{2}$ inch from edge. Leave about $1\frac{1}{2}$ inches of space between the chest block and trunk block. Pleat and overlap the excess muslin to fit snugly, thus shaping the waist.

5. Glue, staple, or nail muslin securely on both front and back of trunk block.

ARMS:

1. Cut a 6 by $2\frac{1}{2}$ inch piece of muslin.

2. Lay muslin flat on the work table with the 6 inch sides at top and bottom.

3. Lay a 1 inch long piece of dowel along the bottom edge of the muslin, leaving an equal amount of muslin on each side. See Figure 4.

Figure 4

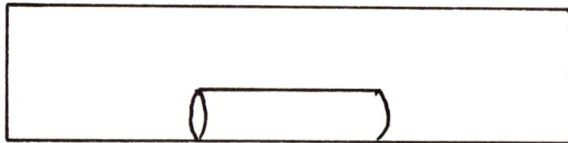

Arm Dowel on Muslin

4. Roll the muslin around the dowel (Figure 5). Be sure the muslin fits snugly.

Figure 5

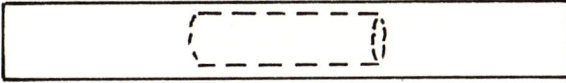

Arm Dowel Rolled in Muslin

5. Staple or nail the muslin on each side of the dowel.
6. Fold down one end of the muslin, about $\frac{1}{2}$ inch. Glue it at the top of the chest block, where the shoulder would be. See Figure 6. For added security, staple or nail it in place.

Figure 6

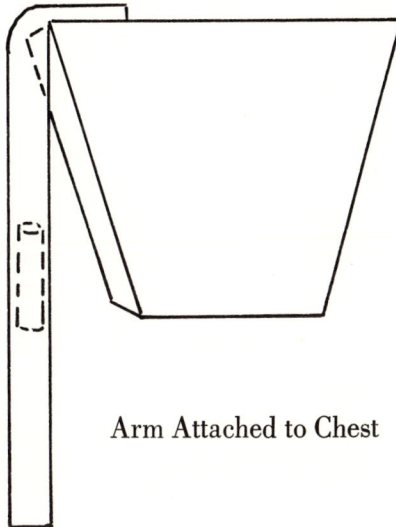

Arm Attached to Chest

7. Follow steps 1 to 6 for the second arm, attaching it to the other side of the chest block.

LEGS:
1. Cut a 5 by $2\frac{1}{2}$ inch piece of muslin.
2. Lay muslin flat on table, with the 5 inch sides at top and bottom.

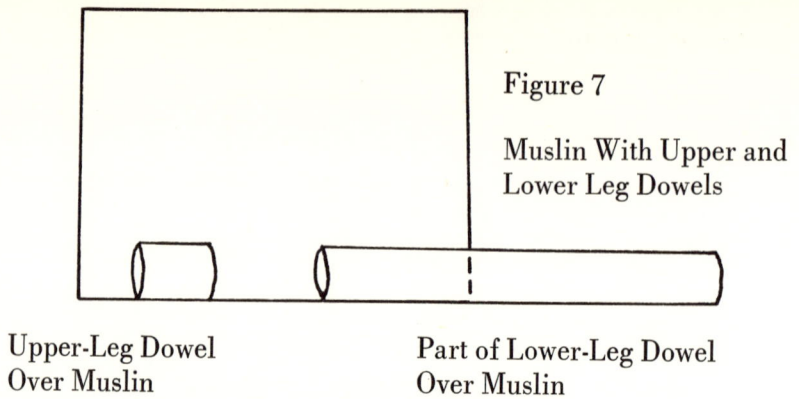

Figure 7

Muslin With Upper and
Lower Leg Dowels

Upper-Leg Dowel
Over Muslin

Part of Lower-Leg Dowel
Over Muslin

Figure 8

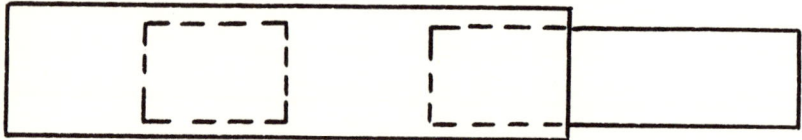

Upper and Lower Leg Dowels Rolled in Muslin

3. Place a 2½ inch long piece of dowel on the lower right edge of the muslin, allowing 1½ inches of the dowel to extend beyond the edge of the cloth (see Figure 7).

4. Lay a 1 inch long piece of dowel on the lower edge of the muslin, leaving a 1 inch space between the longer and the shorter dowels (see Figure 7).

5. Roll the muslin around both dowels, making sure it fits snugly (see Figure 8).

6. Staple or nail the muslin on both sides of each dowel. The space between the muslin-wrapped lower (longer) and upper (shorter) dowels is flexible and can be bent, like a knee.

7. Glue 1 inch of the rolled muslin at the upper leg to the front of the trunk (Figure 9). Staple or nail it securely. Attaching the leg to the front of the trunk rather than the side will allow the marionette's toes to point outward.

8. Follow Steps 1 to 7 for the second leg, attaching it to the other side and front of the trunk block and overlapping the first leg (Figure 9).

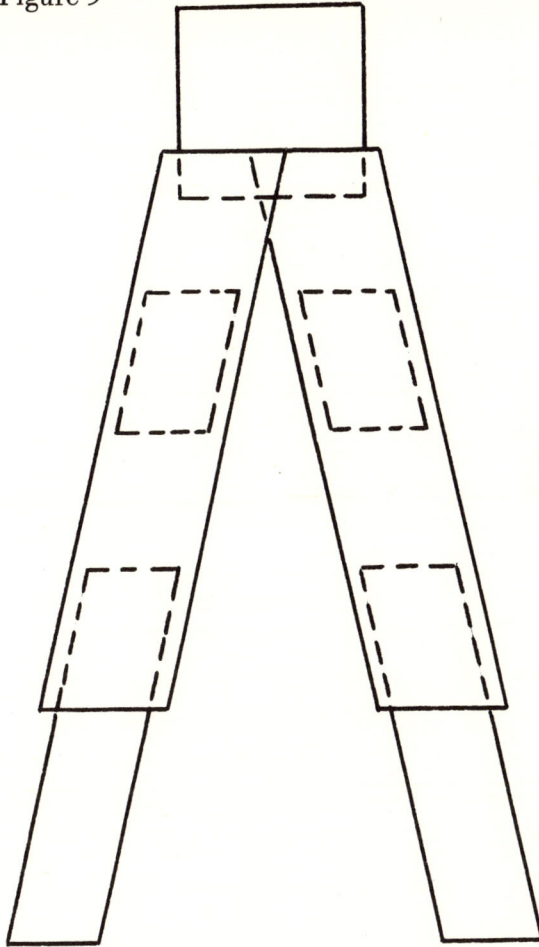

Figure 9

Legs Attached to Trunk Block

The entire figure will be connected as shown in Figure 10. However, the head will not be attached until the figure is dressed. Features will be added after the head is attached.

Dressing the Marionette

Materials:
lightweight bright-green fabric for tunic and cap
lightweight black fabric for hose

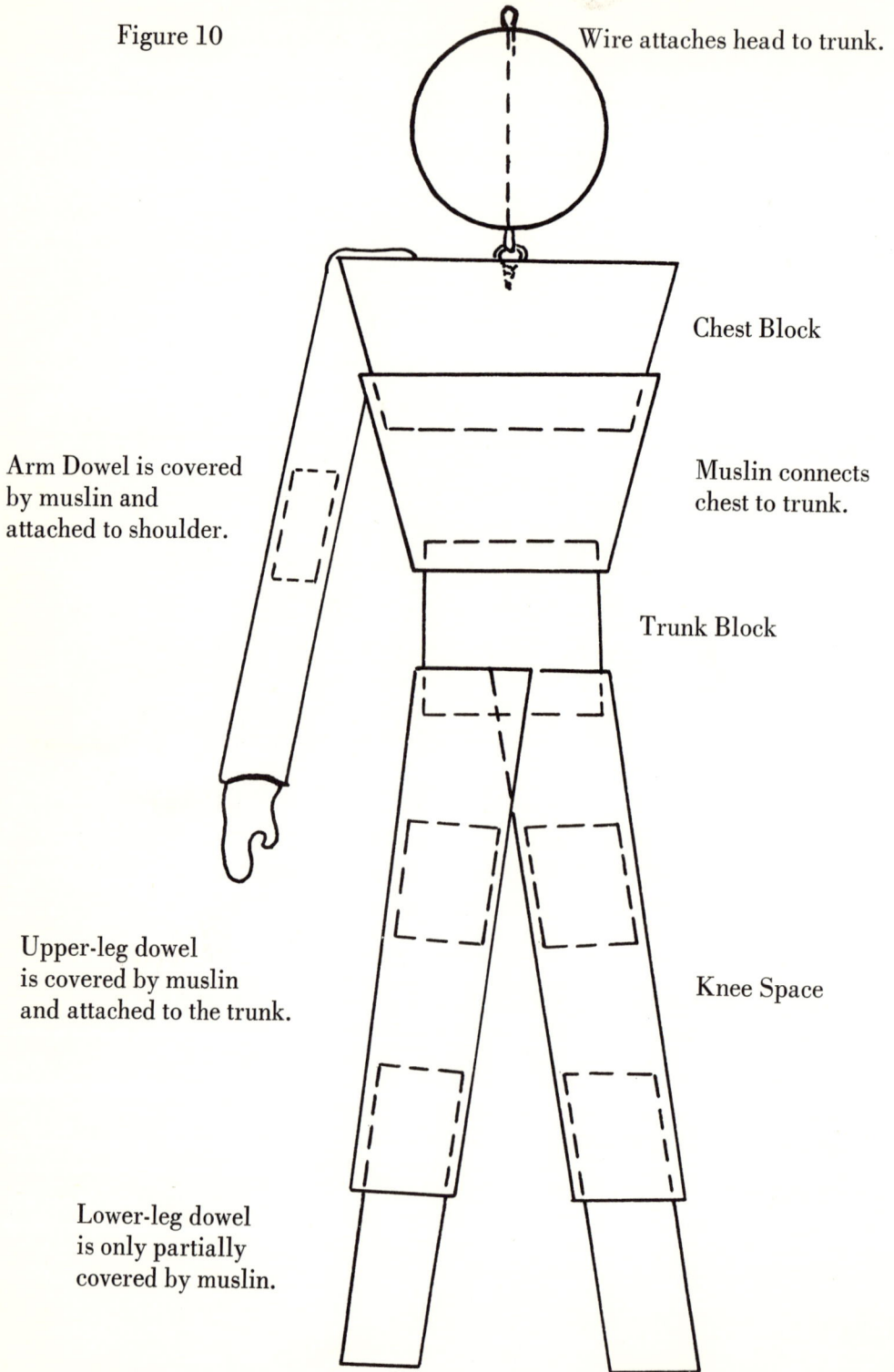

Figure 10

Wire attaches head to trunk.

Chest Block

Arm Dowel is covered
by muslin and
attached to shoulder.

Muslin connects
chest to trunk.

Trunk Block

Upper-leg dowel
is covered by muslin
and attached to the trunk.

Knee Space

Lower-leg dowel
is only partially
covered by muslin.

dark-green felt for boots, collar, mittens, and ears

tracing paper

pencil

scissors

needle, and black and white thread

Directions:

TUNIC:

1. Trace Figure 11 and make a full-sized pattern from it. (See Tracing Directions.)

2. Double the fabric, with the right side in and the wrong side out.

3. Lay the pattern on the doubled fabric, and pin it in place.

4. Cut out the fabric.

5. Remove the pins and the pattern, and you now have both sides of the leprechaun's tunic.

6. Turn down the neck opening 1/4 inch on the wrong side of each half and sew it down with running stitches. Turn down the sleeves 1/4 inch on each half, and sew them down with running stitches.

7. With the wrong sides out, pin the front and back of the tunic together along the shoulders, sleeves, and down the sides.

8. Baste the two halves of the tunic together and remove the pins.

9. Following the basted stitches, sew the sides, shoulders, and sleeves together with running stitches. Remove the basting.

10. Turn the tunic right-side out and iron it.

11. Slip the tunic over the marionette and pull its arms through the sleeves.

12. With a needle and thread tack the tunic to the muslin at the leprechaun's shoulders. Narrow the neck opening, if necessary, with a few tacks.

81

Figure 11

Tunic
Trace and cut out.

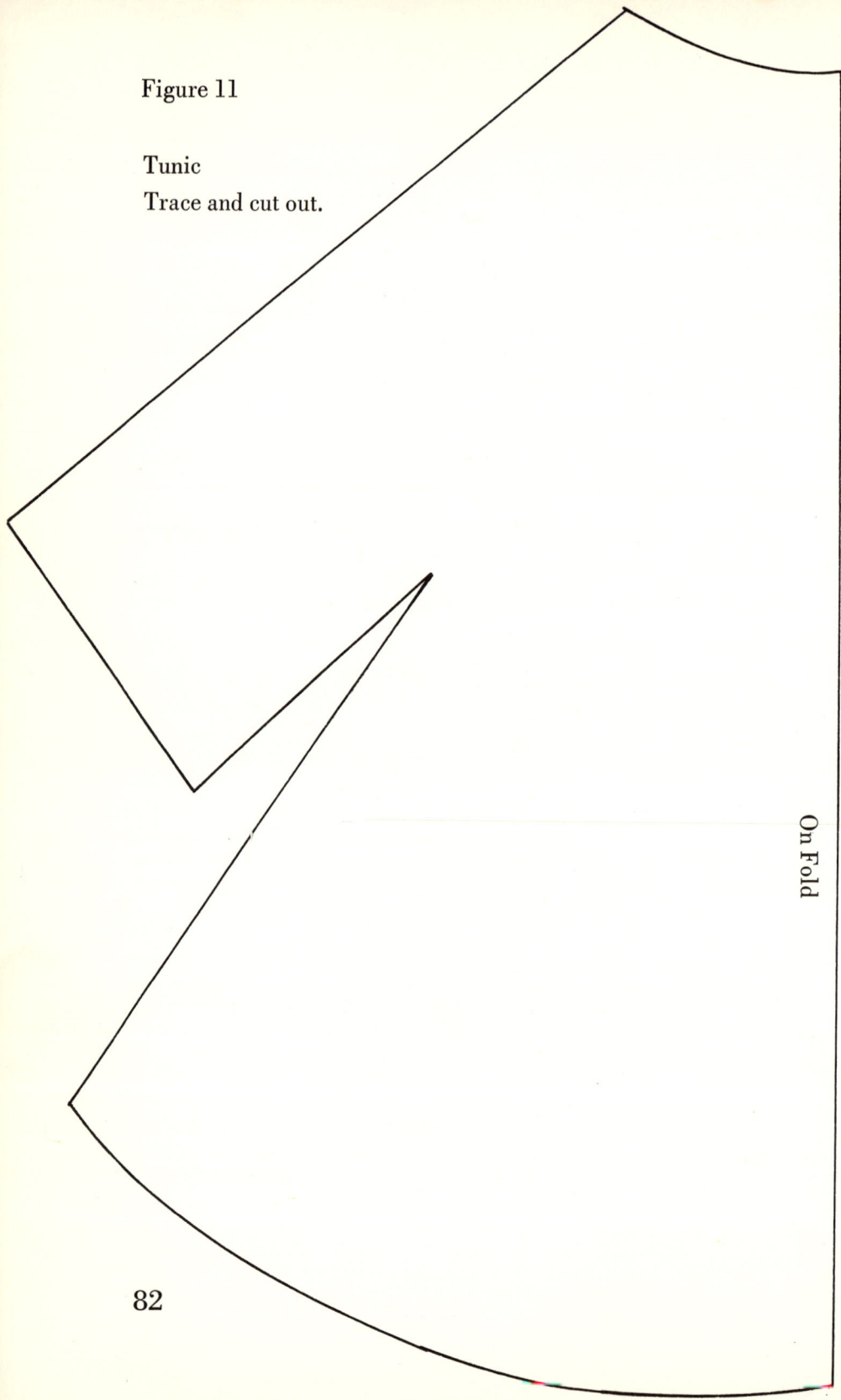

On Fold

82

Figure 12

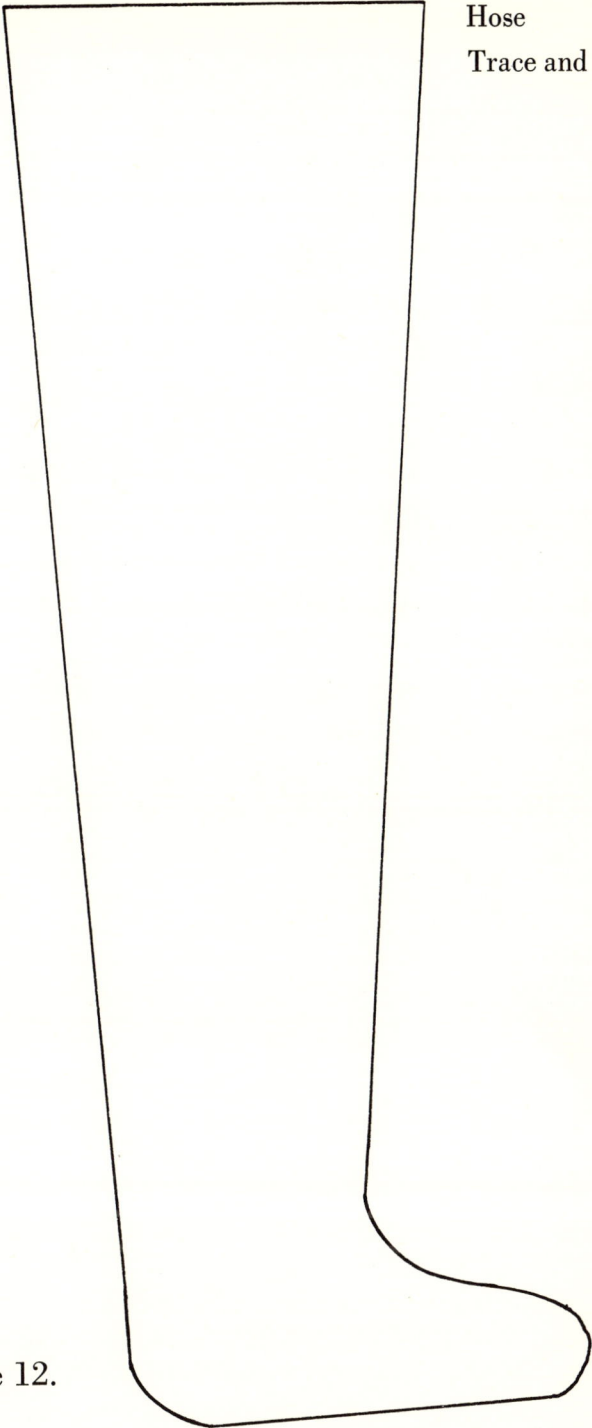

Hose
Trace and cut out.

HOSE:
1. Trace Figure 12.

83

2. Lay the pattern on a doubled piece of black fabric and pin it down.

3. Cut around the pattern. Remove pins and pattern.

4. Turn down the top of each side, ¼ inch, and sew it down with running stitches.

5. With the hem on the outside, pin the two pieces together. Baste, leaving the top open. Remove pins.

6. Sew along the basting with running stitches. Remove basting.

7. Turn hose inside out and iron.

8. Slip the hose over one leg as far as it will go, with the toe pointing outward.

9. Glue the open top of the hose to the muslin and wood.

10. For the second hose, follow steps 2 to 9.

BOOTS:

1. Trace and cut out Figure 13. Follow steps 1 to 4 for making hose, pin the two pieces together, baste, then follow steps 6 to 9 for hose (felt boot does not require a top hem).

2. Slip the boot over one foot as far as it will go, again with the toe pointing outward. Make the second boot.

3. Sew the tops of the boots to the hose, using an overhand stitch.

Figure 13

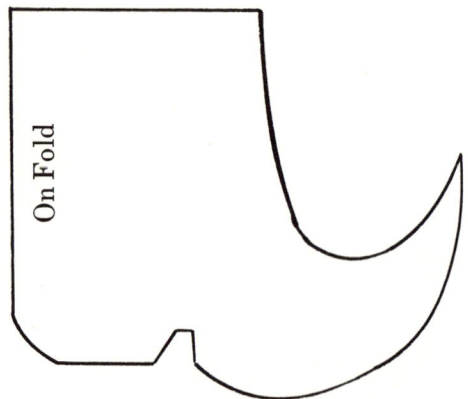

On Fold

Boot

Trace and cut out.

84

Figure 14

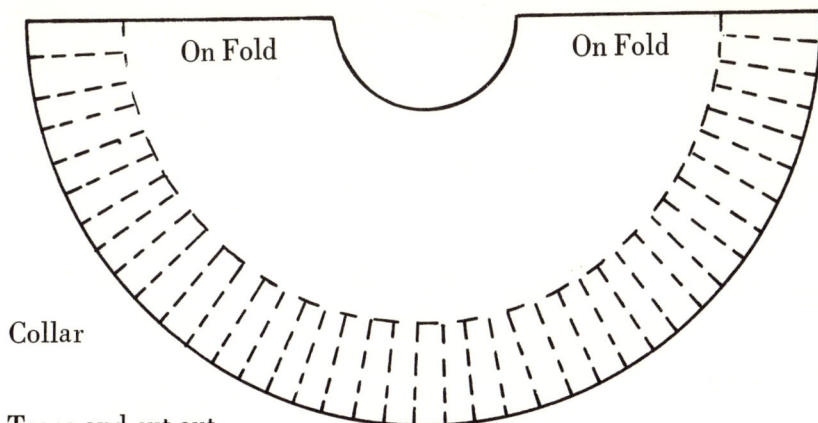

On Fold   On Fold

Collar

Trace and cut out.

Cut dotted line for fringe.

COLLAR:

1. Trace and cut out Figure 14.

2. Lay the pattern on the fold of a doubled piece of green felt and pin it in place.

3. Cut around pattern, but do not cut the fold of the material. Cut dotted lines.

4. Remove pins and pattern.

5. Slip the collar over the marionette's shoulders.

6. With needle and thread, tack the collar to the shoulders of the tunic.

MITTENS:

1. Trace and cut out Figure 15. Transfer to pink or green felt. Pin and cut two mittens. Remove pins.

2. Pin the top of a mitten to bottom of an arm. Sew them together with overhand stitches.

3. Sew the second mitten to the other arm.

85

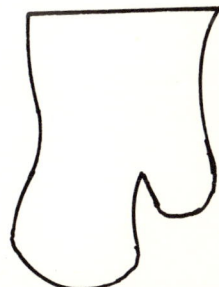

Figure 15

Mitten

Figure 16

Hammer

Figure 17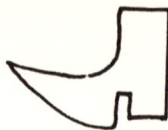

Shoe

HAMMER, SHOE, NEEDLE, AND THREAD FOR WORKING LEPRE-
CHAUNS:

1. Trace Figures 16 and 17. Transfer them to stiff cardboard.
Color them with black ink or crayon.

2. With staples or glue attach the hammer (Figure 16) to
right mitten and the shoe (Figure 17) to the left mitten of
one working leprechaun.

3. Thread a needle. Insert it into the right mitten of the other
working leprechaun, making it look as though he were working
with it. Attach a shoe (Figure 17) to the other mitten with
staples or glue.

CAP:

1. Trace and cut out Figure 18.

2. Transfer the pattern to doubled piece of bright-green
fabric.

3. Pin it and cut it out. Remove pins and pattern.

4. Turn down edge of each bottom opening. Sew edges in
place with small running stitches.

5. Keeping the sewn side of the fabric on the outside, pin both
sides of the cap together. Do not pin the bottom opening.
Baste.

6. Remove pins and sew sides together with small running
stitches. Remove basting.

7. Turn right-side out. Iron if possible.

8. Put the hat aside. It will be attached after the head-control
string is attached to the head.

Figure 18

Pass threaded needle
through cap at x.

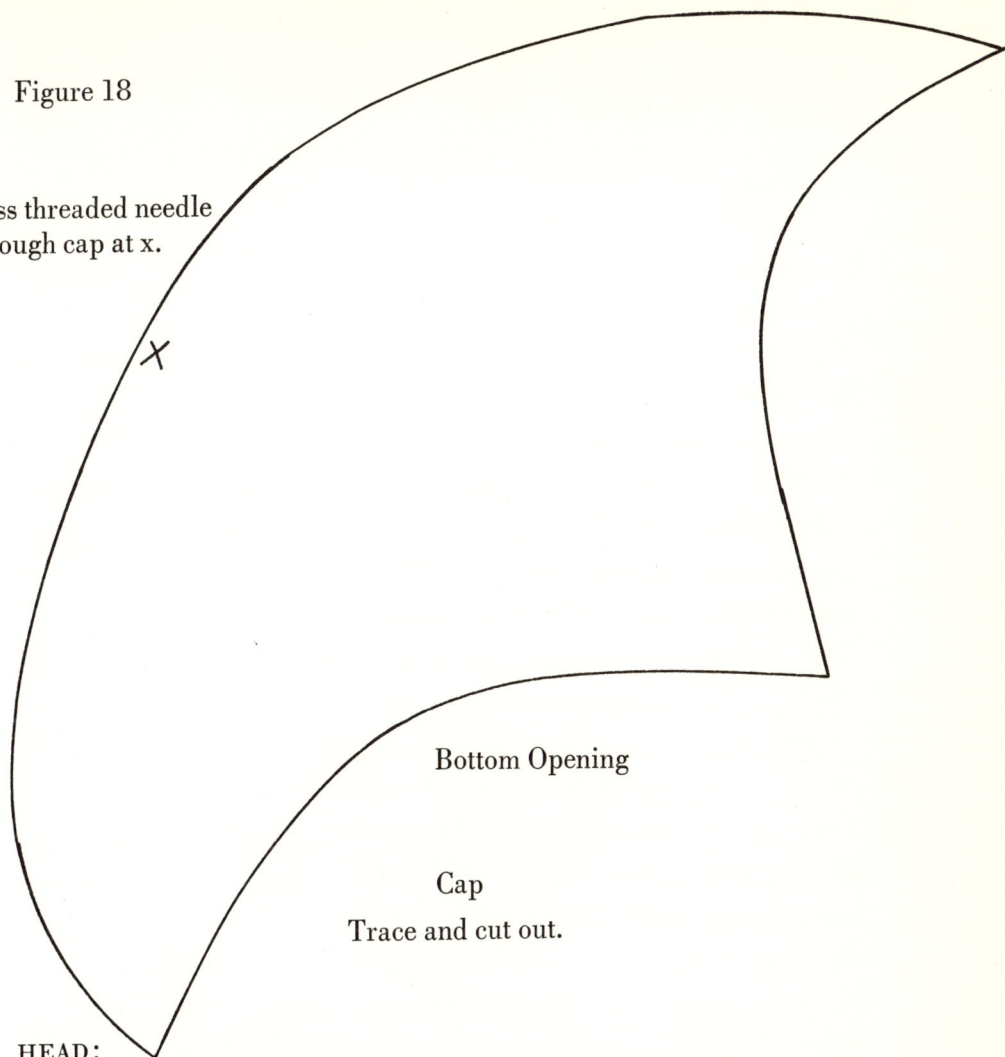

X

Bottom Opening

Cap
Trace and cut out.

HEAD:

1. Apply glue around the upper quarter of the styrofoam ball. Glue one end of black yarn to it while it is still attached to the ball of yarn, and cut the strand to the proper length. Glue, cut, and shape each strand as you go. The hairline should be short over the forehead, for bangs, and longer in back. Tweezers will help you position the yarn as you apply it. This procedure requires patience. Don't worry about the bald spot on the top of the head. The cap will cover it.

87

Figure 19
Eye

Figure 20
Mouth

2. Trace and cut out eyes and mouth (Figures 19 and 20). Use the patterns as templates on black construction paper (see Paper Techniques). Outline in pencil and cut out two eyes and one mouth. Glue the features to the face. Press to hold. Allow to dry.

3. To make a nose, cut a small circle out of black construction paper. Glue it to the face. Hold it in place until it dries.

4. Use red construction paper for cheeks. Cut out two small circles. Glue them on. Press to hold and allow to dry.

5. To attach the head to the body, slip one end of thin wire through the screw eye at the top of the chest block with your fingers or tweezers, and twist and press it into a small loop. Insert other end of wire into the center of the styrofoam ball and out through the top. Allowing for a loop, cut off excess if necessary. Loop the end and press it down into the top of styrofoam to hold. The head is now loosely secured to the body. See Figure 21.

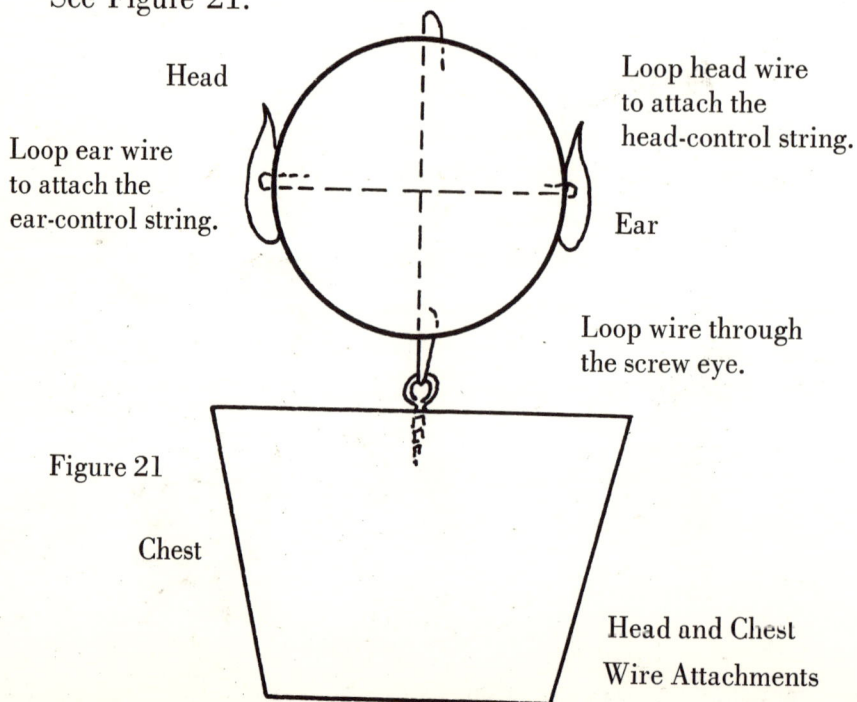

Head

Loop head wire
to attach the
head-control string.

Loop ear wire
to attach the
ear-control string.

Ear

Loop wire through
the screw eye.

Figure 21

Chest

Head and Chest
Wire Attachments

CONTROL STRINGS

Materials:
thin wooden bar, 6 inches by $\frac{3}{4}$ inch, for head control
thin wooden bar, $4\frac{1}{2}$ inches by $\frac{3}{4}$ inch, for leg control
heavy black carpet string
scissors
ruler
wide-eyed needle
thin wire, 6 inches
needle and white thread
straight pins
Elmer's Glue-All
drill

Directions:
1. Before attaching the cap, slip one end of the black carpet string through the wire loop at the top of the head. Tie it securely. The length of the string depends on the height of the puppet-stage opening, since the marionette is manipulated from above the stage. The marionette illustrated has a head string of about 7 inches.
2. Thread the control string attached to the loop at the top of the head through a wide-eyed needle. From the bottom opening of the cap, pass the threaded needle through the top of the cap at approximately the place marked x in Figure 18. Remove needle. This thread becomes the head-control string.
3. Slip the cap over the marionette's head and tack it in place by pushing straight pins through the styrofoam in front, sides, and back. Remove each pin one at a time, and dab glue under the cap. Replace pins. Press to hold, and allow to dry.
4. Drape the tip of the cap to one side of the head and tack it down to the material with a needle and thread.

89

Figure 22

Ear

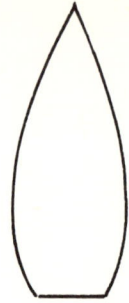

5. Trace and cut out Figure 22, the pointed ear. Place and pin the pattern to green felt. Cut out two ears. Remove the pins and glue one ear to each side of the head. Be sure the ears are positioned over the cap so that they are not hidden. Press to hold, and allow them to dry.

6. Loop one end of the wire. Pass the other end through the base of the right ear, through the styrofoam, and out through the base of the left ear. Pull the wire until the loop at the right ear presses into the styrofoam ball. This secures the ear to the head and provides a loop for stringing.

7. Before looping the wire at the left ear, trim off excess. Make a loop close to the head at this end. Press the loop into the styrofoam ball to secure the second ear to the head. This loop will also be used for stringing.

8. Pass one end of carpet string through the wire loop of one ear and tie it securely. The length of the ear-control string will depend on how high the puppet-stage opening is. The marionette illustrated has a 10 inch ear string.

9. Repeat Step 7 for the second ear.

10. To prepare the 6 inch head-control bar for stringing, drill a small hole in the center. Drill two small holes, each about 1 inch from the center on each side. Drill two more small holes on each end of the bar, about 1 inch from the edges. The head-control bar has five holes, three center holes for the head strings, and two end holes for the hand strings.

90

11. Lay the marionette flat on its back on table. Place the head-control bar on table above the marionette's head. The distance between the two should be as long as the head strings are.

12. Tie the center head-control string through the center hole on control bar.

13. Tie each ear-control string through holes on the control bar at each side of head string. Be sure the three strings are equal in length.

14. Thread a wide-eyed needle with carpet string. The length should be a little more than the distance between the marionette's hand and the head-control bar. Knot one end of the thread, and pass the needle through the upper hand and sleeve with the knot at the back. The marionette shown has a 13 inch hand string. Remove the needle from the string.

15. Repeat Step 13 for the second hand string.

16. With the marionette fully extended on the table, tie the loose end of the hand string through the last hole at the edge of the head-control bar.

17. Repeat Step 15 for the second hand string. Be sure both hand strings are of equal length. Now the head-control bar has five strings attached; one head, two ear, and two hand strings. Trim loose ends if necessary.

LEG-CONTROL BAR:

1. To prepare the 4½ inch leg-control bar for stringing, drill two small holes about 1 inch from each edge.

2. Lay the leg-control bar under the head bar.

3. Thread carpet string through wide-eyed needle. Knot one end. Pass the needle through toe of the boot with the knot in back. The marionette shown has a 23 inch leg string.

4. Repeat this step for the second leg.

5. Keeping the marionette flat on table, pass the loose end

91

of the leg string through the corresponding hole in leg control bar.

6. Repeat this for the second leg. Be sure leg strings are of equal length. Now the leg-control bar has two strings attached, one for the left leg, and one for the right leg. Trim loose ends if necessary. See Figure 23.

Suggested Variations for Making Other Marionettes:
1. Instead of dowels, you may want to use a coat-hanger roll cut to size for the arms and legs. The muslin is attached exactly the same way.
2. Instead of a styrofoam ball for the head, make one of papier-maché.
3. Experiment with different-sized empty wooden spools of thread or any kind of spring wire for the various parts of the body.
4. You may want to use a square block of wood without features for the head. It might also be fun to use these mario-nettes without dressing them.
5. You may also dress marionettes with discarded fabric from a scrap box. Decorate them with rickrack or other suitable trimming.
6. You may want to give your leprechauns beards consisting of strands of wool or crepe paper.
7. Try nylon fish line instead of black carpet thread for controling marionettes. This would make the control strings invisible. You can make your marionette any way you like, as long as it moves.

Suggestions for Making the Other Puppets:
1. The king may be a hand puppet, with a head made from a nylon stocking, a styrofoam ball, or papier-maché. For the nylon-stocking head, see instructions for the Pilgrim Man, in "Unexpected Guests." For a styrofoam hand puppet, see instructions for making the mailman in "A Surprise for

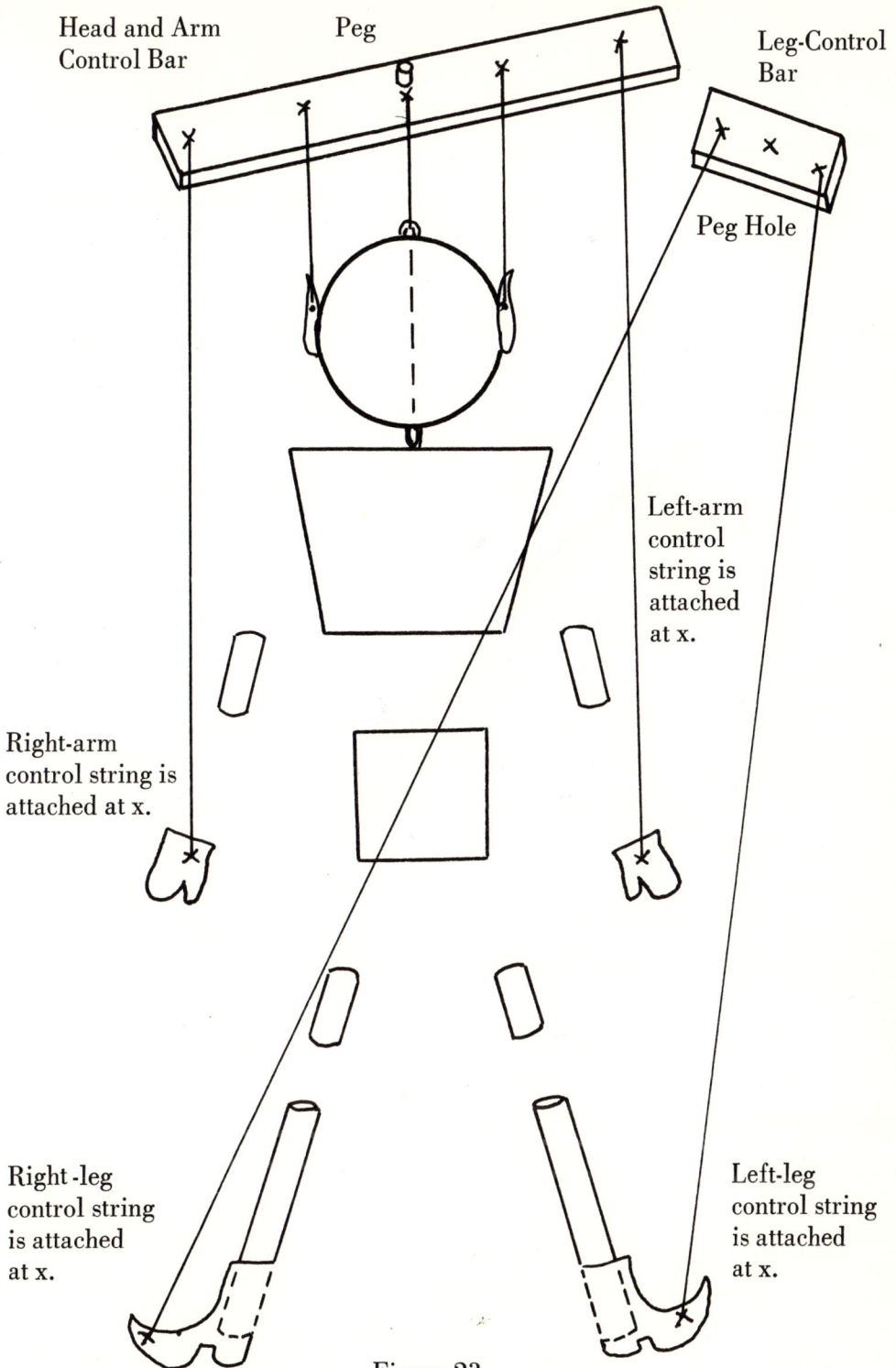

Head and Arm Control Bar

Peg

Leg-Control Bar

Peg Hole

Left-arm control string is attached at x.

Right-arm control string is attached at x.

Right-leg control string is attached at x.

Left-leg control string is attached at x.

Figure 23

Strings Attached to Control Bars

Mr. Winkle." Instructions for making papier-maché appear in *Hand Puppets: How to Make and Use Them* (see Further Reading List).

2. The herald can be made the same way as the one in "The First Easter Eggs," substituting a trumpet for a drum. Make only one herald.

Holding the Marionette for Action:

1. Hold the head-control bar in your left hand and the leg-control bar in your right hand in front of the head bar. The marionette is now standing in a natural position.

2. To move the legs, tilt the leg bar from right to left, or move the leg strings one at a time with the fingers of your right hand.

3. Tilt the head-control bar in your left hand to move the head.

4. When the lazy leprechaun dances a jig, hold the marionette upright and move only the leg-control bar. When he lies down, rest his body on the floor by lowering the head-control bar. Jiggle first one string of the leg bar, then the other, to make his toes wiggle.

5. When the working marionettes are hammering and sewing, lower their bodies to sitting positions and move the hand strings on the head bars.

Every puppeteer develops his own techniques for moving the marionette through practice.

When the marionette is not in action, hang it on the wall so that the strings will not get tangled. To do his, nail a small peg above the center string on the head-control bar. Make a hole in the center of leg-control bar that is large enough to fit the peg. Rest the leg bar over the head bar by fitting the hole through the peg. Now the marionette hangs in a natural position and can be hung over a nail on a wall.

94

Production Notes

Technique:

A narrator reads the story, while the puppets enact it. The action and the narration should be carefully synchronized.

Cast:

Liam, the lazy leprechaun
two working leprechauns
king
herald
narrator

Marionette Stage:

Since a marionette is moved by control strings, the puppeteer manipulating the strings must stand above the puppet. This requires a stage designed to permit this kind of control.

An elaborate, professional stage has a high valance, behind which the puppeteer stands on a high bridge. The valance masks him from the view of the audience.

However, your marionette stage can be very simple and you can perform effectively before the audience. Draw a curtain across a framework attached to a tabletop. A curtain can also be drawn on a cord attached to the sides of an open doorway or the walls of a room, with a table in front of it.

The puppeteer stands on a chair behind the curtain and is seen only from the waist up. Do not be concerned about distracting the audience. The important thing is what the marionette does on stage.

Opaque cloth is recommended for the curtain, so that nothing can be seen through it, especially with a light shining on the stage. You can also stand behind an awning or canvas.

To perform with the king hand puppet and herald push-

96

puppet, the puppeteer thrusts his hand under the curtain from below the stage. This is also done with the moon-rod prop. They exit in the same manner.

Scenery and Properties:

A forest is pointed on the backdrop attached to the curtain. A few trees are fastened to the floor. One of them has a large limb extending across the stage, which is sturdy enough to hold Liam when he climbs it. In the nighttime scene, a blue light shines on the stage. A cardboard disk, 5 inches in diameter, covered with aluminum foil and attached to a long narrow rod, represents the full moon. At dawn a red light shines on the stage. A pile of small cardboard shoes is quickly placed on the stage between the blue and red lighting periods. Two small bags are needed, which are carried by the king in the end.

Action:

The action takes place in a forest clearing. When the narrator explains who the leprechauns are, be sure that two busy leprechauns are hammering and sewing with proper sound effects. Liam lies on his back. The sound effects in this story are important. Someone behind the stage whistles, hums, claps, and sings. When Liam climbs the tree, place him on the limb. After the sleeping leprechauns awake, their movements are slow. On the night of the Princess's wedding, a puppeteer below stage handles the full moon prop with the blue light shining on it, while the leprechauns dance by moonlight. It would be interesting, in the end, to draw the curtain to the strains of a wedding march while the leprechauns are dancing.

PURIM

Queen Esther Saves Her People

DOROTHY ZELIGS

Of all the Jewish holidays, Purim is one of the merriest and happiest. It celebrates the day when, centuries ago, the Jews were saved by their beautiful Queen Esther from being massacred by the Persians.

It is not observed as a religious holiday as Jewish festivals are. Instead, a gay carnival-like spirit prevails, particularly among the children.

On the eve of Purim, the synagogue is crowded for the reading from the Book of Esther. The children have rattles made of wood and tin. Whenever the name of Haman is mentioned, there is a great burst of noise to show disapproval of this wicked man.

Purim began in Persia, now known as Iran. Today it is a specially important festival to the Jews living in Israel. In front of the Opera House in Tel Aviv, a platform is erected. There, a scene from the story of Purim is enacted. The actors usually make all the characters look and act comical. Even Queen Esther is apt to walk with an exaggerated stride.

In the evening, after services, the streets are crowded with people dressed in costumes, wearing masks of all kinds, singing, and making noise with rattles and horns.

Reprinted from *The Story of Jewish Holidays and Customs*, by Dorothy Zeligs, published by Bloch Publishing Co., 1942. Used by permission.

98

The story that follows is best enacted as a live pantomime with the actors wearing masks and appropriate costumes.

Scene I

Narrator: King Ahasuerus, ruler of the mighty Persian empire, sat upon his throne. He had banished his beautiful wife, Vashti, from the throne because she had dared to disobey him. Now he was choosing a new queen.

Many beautifully dressed maidens had been summoned to pass before the king for his royal inspection. One by one they approached him and bowed before him.

Among the maidens was the beautiful young Jewess, Esther. She had been an orphan from early childhood and had been brought up by Mordecai, her uncle, who loved her as if she were his own daughter.

Of all the lovely maidens, Esther was the most pleasing in the eyes of the king and so he chose her to be his new queen.

Scene II

Narrator: Mordecai, who frequently sat at the gate of the king's palace, overheard two guardsmen who plotted to harm the king. Mordecai told Esther of the plot and she warned the king. The two plotters were punished.

Scene III

Narrator: Now, the king had a prime minister, a proud and haughty man. He expected that all should bow before him and do him honor. But Mordecai, the Jew, who sat at the palace gate, would not bow before Haman.

Then in a great rage Haman vowed that he would be revenged, not only upon Mordecai, but upon all the Jews throughout the Persian empire.

Then Haman cunningly influenced the king to issue a
decree ordering that all the Jews should be put to death
on a certain day.

There was great mourning among the Jews. Mordecai
was in despair. He told Esther that it was her duty to save
her people. Perhaps it was for this very purpose that she
had been raised to her high position.

Esther sorrowfully reminded her uncle of the Persian law
that no one dared to appear before the king without being
summoned. Anyone who disobeyed this law was put to
death unless the king held out his golden scepter, as a
sign that the person's life was spared. And Esther told
Mordecai that the king had not sent for her for the past
thirty days.

But Esther was convinced by her uncle that she must
have courage and appear before the king to plead for her
people.

Esther, dressed in her most beautiful gown, entered the
great inner court, where the king sat. And he held out the
golden scepter that was in his hand, for Esther found favor
in his eyes. Then Esther drew near and touched the top
of the scepter. And the king said:

King: What wilt thou, Queen Esther? For whatever thy
request, even to the half of the kingdom, it shall be given
thee.

Narrator: And Esther said:

Esther: If it seems good unto the king, let the king and
Haman come tomorrow to the banquet that I have prepared
for him.

Narrator: The king agreed to do so.

Scene IV

Narrator: The following day, Queen Esther entertained King

100

Ahasuerus and Haman at a banquet in her apartment. How proud Haman was at being honored in this way! The king was in a good mood and he said to his beautiful queen:

King: Whatever thy petition, it shall be granted thee, and whatever thy request, even to the half of the kingdom, it shall be performed.

Narrator: Then Esther answered and said:

Esther: If I have found favor in thy sight, O king, and if it pleases the king, let my life be given me and my people, for we are to be destroyed.

Narrator: Then Ahasuerus said to the queen:

King: Who is he and where is he that dares to do this evil deed?

Narrator: Then Esther replied:

Esther: An adversary and an enemy, even this wicked Haman.

Narrator: Then Haman was terrified before the king and queen and pleaded for his life.

But Haman was punished by the king, and the lives of the Jewish people were spared.

And Mordecai was honored and made next in power to the king.

Mask for Queen Esther

Materials:

construction paper, 12 by 14 inches, for a basic pattern

white construction paper or Bristol drawing paper, 12 by 14 inches, for a finished mask

three pieces of construction paper of any color, 5 by 18 inches, for hair

Scotch tape

scissors

pencil
ruler

Directions:

1. To make a basic pattern, fold the 12 inch side of the construction paper in half.

2. Open and place construction paper over your face, with the center fold vertical, dividing your face from forehead to chin.

3. Work with only one side of the paper. Starting at the center of the chin, draw around your jaw to the bottom of the ear. Continue making the curved line out to the edge of the paper. This will become the edge of the headband. If you find it difficult to do this yourself, have another person draw a line on the paper.

4. Starting over the fold, draw the top line along the forehead, about 2½ inches beyond the hairline, and curve it gradually towards the hairline at the temple.

5. For the upper edge of the headband, follow this line, making it parallel to the lower edge of the headband. The headband will be about 3 by 2 inches. It will not be enough to go around the head, but it will be a start.

6. Locate eye, nose, and mouth with your fingers, while a second person marks them with a pencil.

7. Remove the construction paper from your face. Only half of the facial contour lines have been drawn. Fold the construction paper in half again, and retrace the drawn lines, shaping and defining them. Carefully, sketch in the eye, half of the nose and the upper and lower lips.

8. Cut along the contour lines.

9. Cut along the *lower* half of the eye, preferably with curved scissors. Cut the nose and upper and lower lip.

10. Open the paper. The two sides are exactly alike.

11. Draw a V-shaped notch at the top center of the mask, extending it downward about $2\frac{1}{2}$ inches.

12. Draw slightly smaller notches at each jaw and the chin.

13. Fold the mask in half again and cut the notches into both sides. Open paper and carefully make necessary adjustments.

14. This basic pattern is to be used as a template (see Paper Techniques).

15. Fold a piece of white construction paper or Bristol drawing paper to make the finished mask, as you did the basic pattern. Fold the pattern again and lay it on the fold of the new paper. Trace around the contour lines. Trace all cut-out features. Remove the template.

16. Keeping the new paper folded, cut the contour lines. Cut the lower half of the eyes, the nose, and upper and lower lips with small curved scissors.

17. Open the new mask. Bend down the lower half of the eyes. Slit and fringe the upper half.

18. Shape the mask to fit your face. To do this, overlap the V-shaped notches as little or as much as necessary. Close them and hold them together with Scotch tape. This gives the basic mask depth to fit over your face. See Figure 1.

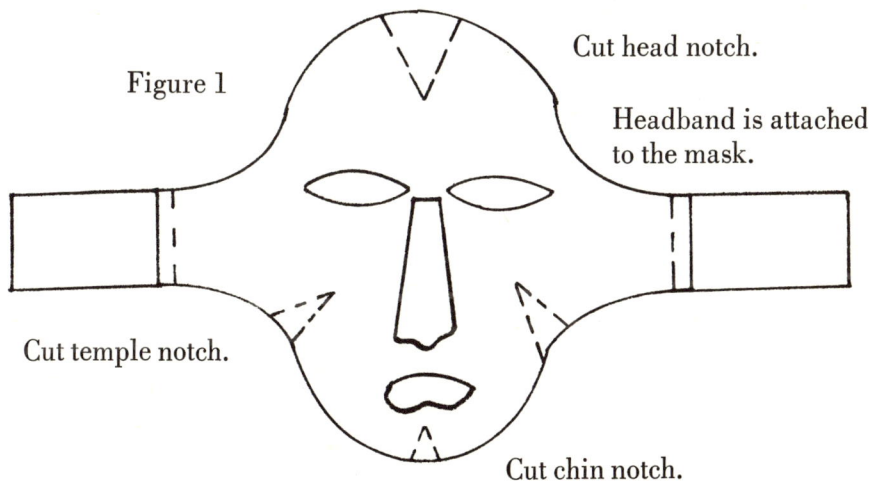

Figure 1

Cut head notch.

Headband is attached to the mask.

Cut temple notch.

Cut chin notch.

Mask With Features

Cut out nose, mouth, and lower half of eyes.

19. The paper headbands are not long enough to go around your head. Add another piece of construction paper to each, making it the same width and as long as necessary to fit around your head. Be sure each piece is long enough to allow for overlapping at the temples and at the back. Overlap and glue them together with Scotch tape.

HAIR:

1. Use construction paper about 5 inches wide and 18 inches long.

2. Cut one short end of this piece into strips about ½ inch wide and 4 inches long. Cut the other short end into strips about ½ inch wide and 10 inches long. Curl both ends (see Paper Techniques).

3. Drape the 5 inch side over the forehead of the mask for bangs, and attach it with Scotch tape. The other end will drape over the headband and down the back.

4. Prepare two similar pieces of the same size, cutting and curling 10 inch long strips at one end only to make the hair at the sides of the mask.

5. Attach the uncurled edge of each side piece over the top center of the piece that goes over the head, allowing curled end to drape down at each side of mask. This forms the left and right sides of the hair.

Suggestions for Making Other Masks in the Story:

Construct masks for the other characters in basically the same way as for Queen Esther. Vary decorations to distinguish King Ahasuerus from Haman. Be sure that all masks have *open* mouths to look as though they are talking.

The king's mask should have a black curled beard and sideburns. Make a gold crown to set on his head (instructions for making a king's crown are given for the king puppet in

"The Three Kings," or create your own crown to fit over your head).

Make Haman's beard by slashing red construction paper into points. Fringe one side of the construction paper, and glue it to the chin. Do the same for Haman's hair, making it stand upright. This will give him a comical appearance.

Using the Masks for Action:
Slip the mask over your head, with the headband fitting snugly around the back. The eyes, nose, and mouth should fit over yours to allow you to see, breathe, and speak through the openings. Now you are transformed into another character.

Production Notes

Technique:
A narrator reads the story. The dialogue is spoken by each character. Live puppets, wearing masks, pantomime the actions in full view of the audience. The action and narration should be carefully synchronized, the actor performing while the narrator tells the story.

Cast:
narrator
King Ahasuerus
several Jewish maidens
Queen Esther
Mordecai
Haman
two guardsmen
several Jewish people in the background
two king's men

Scenery and Properties:
No elaborate scenery is necessary. A simple backdrop may be

used with Persian castles painted on it to identify the place of the action. The only properties needed are a chair for the king's throne, a golden scepter, and a table and chairs, for the banquet.

106

Action:

Since Purim is a fun holiday, remember to be as comical and exaggerated in your movements as possible. Actions should be spontaneous. Improvise as you go along, to achieve an un-studied funny mood.

Scene I takes place in the king's throne room. He is seated on a chair, while maidens approach, one-by-one, and bow before him. Some trip over their long gowns; others stride in awkwardly. Esther is the last to appear. She could be a boy dressed as a queen and pretending to be very coquettish but awkward. She exaggerates her coyness when she is chosen by the king. He does this by tapping her on the shoulder with his scepter.

Scene II takes place at the palace gate, and can be performed near a stage exit. Two guardsmen whisper to each other. Mordecai stealthily approaches and listens. Then he runs through the opposite exit to warn Esther, who is not seen. When the plotters are punished, two of the king's men appear and drag the guardsmen off.

Scene III takes place at the palace gate and is also performed at a stage exit. Mordecai is seen sitting near the exit. Haman struts in pompously. He approaches Mordecai, and with gestures orders Mordecai to bow before him. Mordecai refuses by turning his head away. Haman shakes his fist in rage and threatens Mordecai, pointing his finger at him. He sweeps his arms around, signifying that he will also bring doom upon the Jewish people, who can be seen in the background. All exit.

Several Jewish people enter and are seen wailing. Mordecai enters and wrings his hands in despair. When he goes to inform Esther, all exit.

Esther and Mordecai enter, and we see the uncle talking to

the queen. She shakes her head and throws up her arms, signifying that she can do nothing. But Mordecai persists and convinces Esther, who nods her head. They exit together.

The king and queen enter. The king holds his scepter out to Esther, who touches it.

Scene IV takes place in the banquet room. The king, queen, and Haman are seated at the banquet table. Haman, flattered at being invited, throws out his chest and nods his head. After the king and queen converse, she points an accusing finger at Haman, who cringes, falls to his knees and pleads for his life with upraised folded hands. Soon two of the king's men enter and drag Haman away.

Several Jewish people enter in a jubilant mood and embrace one another. Mordecai walks to the king's side, while Queen Esther embraces her husband.

EASTER

The First Easter Eggs

R O W E N A   B E N N E T T

Characters:
Rabbit
Hen
Turkey
Goose
Herald
Little Bird
King

Properties:
trees
three small nests

At Curtain Rise:
Hen, Turkey and Goose come in. Rabbit follows them, carrying a market basket.

Rabbit (*calling in a tired voice*):
　　Sweet cane to sell! And berry juice!
　　Come buy, oh hen and goose.

Sweet sugar cane and berry juice.
(*The barnyard fowl turn and look at him.*)

Hen:

Go 'way, you bumpkin. Do not meddle
With hens and chickens. You cannot peddle
The juice or berries or sugar cane
To barnyard fowl so rich in grain.

Turkey (*haughtily*):

We've golden corn and golden meal.
You've naught at all that could appeal
To folks like us . . .

Goose:

Unless you sold
Something golder than corn is gold.
*(They turn their backs on Rabbit. The tired Rabbit sighs.
The Herald enters. He stands at the extreme left of the
stage, front, and beats on his drum. Hen, Goose, Turkey
and Rabbit turn toward him.)*

Herald:

Oh, I am the herald of the king!
Oh, hear ye, one and all!
The good king sends a message to
His subjects, great and small.

Turkey:

Hear! Hear! Hear!

Herald:

The king is weary of water and wine,
The king is tired of meat—
Of the wild boar's head and chicken legs,
And what he wants is some good fresh eggs,
Some good fresh eggs to eat.

Hen (*excitedly*):

Hear! Hear! Hear!

110

Herald:

A good fresh egg is hard to get
In the early spring when the fields are wet
And this is the thing you must all be told:
The good king offers a bag of gold
To the one who brings him from east or west
The finest eggs in the finest nest.

Goose (*to other fowl with enthusiasm*):

Did you hear *that*, friends?
What a piece of luck!

Turkey:

Oh, gobble!

Goose:

Oh, honk!

Hen:

Oh, cluck, cluck, cluck!

Herald:

To the one who brings from the north or south
Eggs that will water a monarch's mouth
Ere the Easter day begins to lag
Will be given gold in a bulging bag.

(He exits. Hen, Turkey and Goose move to the front of the stage. The Rabbit follows but keeps his distance.)

Goose (*exclaiming*):

My! What a message!

Turkey (*grandly*):

It makes me perky.
There are no eggs like the eggs of the turkey.

Goose:

You're going to do what the king has bidden?

Turkey (*smugly*):

I'll get my eggs in the nest that's hidden
Down by the hedgerow. Then

111

I'll carry them safely straight to the king.
I'm bound to be winning the bag of gold.
I guess there's no one who needs to be told
That the King's an epicure who knows what's best—
And turkey eggs lead all the rest!
(*Turkey exits haughtily.*)

Rabbit (*looking after her and sighing hopelessly*):
My! What a barnyard snob *that* bird is!

Goose (*to Hen*):
I really don't know how good her word is
She *may* get the prize if she's *very* lucky.
Her eggs are big. But they just *aren't* goosey.
You and I may be waders and wobblers . . .
But our eggs are better than that old gobbler's.

Hen:
And so they are. I'm all in a flurry
To get my eggs to the king in a hurry. (*They start off stage but the Rabbit intervenes.*)

Rabbit:
I've just one question. Please let me ask it.
When you've won the gold, will you buy from my basket?

Goose:
Oh, don't be silly!
We'll be too grand . . .

Hen:
To talk to a peddler and poor farm hand. (*They go off.*)

Rabbit (*sobbing loudly*):
Oh, isn't there some one to understand? (*Little Bird enters. He flys around Rabbit once or twice.*)

Bird (*as he flys*):
Oh, dear! Oh, dear! What have we here?
Please, little rabbit, dry your tear. (*He alights on the ground and sits in front of the Rabbit.*)

Rabbit (*between sobs*):

There are no beans stored up in our beanery,
And the good spring greens haven't come with their green
ery . . .

Bird (*sympathetically*):

I know. And the snow still chills the scenery.

Rabbit:

My mommy is working her hands to blisters
Trying to care for my brothers and sisters
But our rabbit hole, from cellar to garret,
Holds nary a nibble of cabbage or carrot.
And the barnyard fowl, they put on such airs
That I just can't sell my poor little wares.

Bird:

Then why not try for the bag of gold
The king has offered (*for eggs, I'm told*)
It would rescue your family from hunger and cold.

Rabbit:

Oh I'd love to try, but it's quite absurd.
I can't lay an egg, for I'm not a bird.
I can't do a thing for the prize, I'm afraid:
Eggs are a product that must be *laid*.

Bird:

Nonsense! They're something that can be *made*.
Nowadays it's all in the making
Whether it's brewing, or boiling, or baking;
Whether it's welded, or glued, or cemented,
There's nothing that cannot be *made* or *invented*.

Rabbit:

I see what you mean. I get your suggestion.
Oh, what can *I* make?

Bird:

Yes. That is the question.

113

Rabbit:

Well, I know of *one* thing at which I am handy.

It's making a panful of good sugar candy.

Bird:

Hurrah! Just the thing. Now get up, and cheer up.

Do you see, over yonder, that kettle of syrup? (*He turns toward offstage.*)

Rabbit:

I see it quite clearly. You've made things so plain.

I'll make *candy* eggs of my sweetening cane.

Bird:

And add maple syrup not spoiled by the rain.

Rabbit (*excitedly*):

I'll color them gaily with berry juice stain.

What fun it will be!

Bird:

I hope it will bring

Pleasure for you and a prize from the king.

(*Rabbit and Bird exit. There is a short silence, and then a tumult of honks, clucks and gobbles is heard offstage. The Goose, Hen and Turkey enter quarreling. Each of them has a nest of eggs, and they talk so fast that they all seem to be talking at once.*)

Goose:

My eggs are whitest.

Hen:

Mine shine the most . . .

Turkey:

No, mine are brightest. (*They begin shouting and squawking at each other.*)

Goose:

Don't shout, you clout . . .

Hen:

Don't talk so loud. (*They begin pushing and bumping each other.*)

Goose:

Don't push!

Hen:

Don't crush!

Turkey:

Don't crowd! (*They get rougher and rougher.*)

Goose (*half crying*):

You've hurt my wings.

Turkey (*angrily*):

You've bruised my legs!

(*They all push and shove, and their nests turn over and the eggs spill out.*)

Hen (*wailing*):

Oh, my! There go our precious eggs! They're all broken.

(*King and Herald enter.*)

King (*looking at broken eggs*):

What's this? What's this? I never saw

Such rioting. It is the law

To make arrests of those who riot

So next time none of them will try it.

Goose (*pleadingly*):

Please, sir, we tried to suit your diet,

By fetching, as we ran or rambled,

The best fresh eggs—but *now* they're *scrambled!*

King (*angrily*):

I don't like scrambled eggs at all.

Why did you ever let them fall?

Rabbit (*entering and going up to King with his basket of eggs*):

I've overcome my rabbit shyness
To bring these eggs, Your Royal Highness.

King (*taking a jelly bean from the rabbit's basket and holding it out for all to see*):
What eggs are these? I've never seen
Bright colored ones, all red and green
And blue and yellow, on Easter Day. (*He nibbles it, then bites it.*)
Upon my word! The taste is sweet!
They're good to see, and good to eat. (*He samples more.*)
Friend rabbit, let's not be too hasty,
Tell me what makes these eggs so tasty.

Rabbit (*happily*):
They're made with sweetest sugar cane
And maple sugar, smoothest grain
And colored with a berry stain.

King:
Some day you'll have to tell to me
The very secret recipe.

Rabbit:
Oh, do not praise, and do not scold me
It was a little bird who told me.

King:
At any rate, my thanks, tenfold:
And here, sir, is your bag of gold. (*He hangs bag over Rabbit's arm.*)

Rabbit (*happily*):
My mother and my little sisters
No more will wear their paws to blisters,
And rich will be my little brothers,
My aunts, my cousins and the others.

116

Our rabbit holes and all our garrets,
Will overflow with peas and carrots.
King (*to Rabbit who goes toward door*):
I like your eggs; they're sweet as honey.
Come back next year, good Easter Bunny.
(*All cheer, Hurrah! Hurrah! Hurrah! as the curtain closes.*)

Hen Push-Puppet

Materials:

poster board for body, color of your choice
construction paper, color of your choice, for wings; bright-red
    for crest and wattles
tracing paper
ruler
pencil
scissors
Elmer's Glue-All
white thread
wooden board, about $2\frac{1}{2}$ by 10 inches

Directions:

BODY:

1. Trace Figures 1 to 5 to make patterns for the hen's body, tail, wings, crest, wattle, and eye lining (see Tracing Directions). Use poster board of any color for the body. The tail, also made of poster board, should be the same color as the body. The wings should be made of construction paper of any color. Use bright-red construction paper for the crest and wattles. The eye lining should be made of construction paper of the same color as the body. Cut all solid lines. Score and bend dotted lines (see Paper Techniques, Scoring).

117

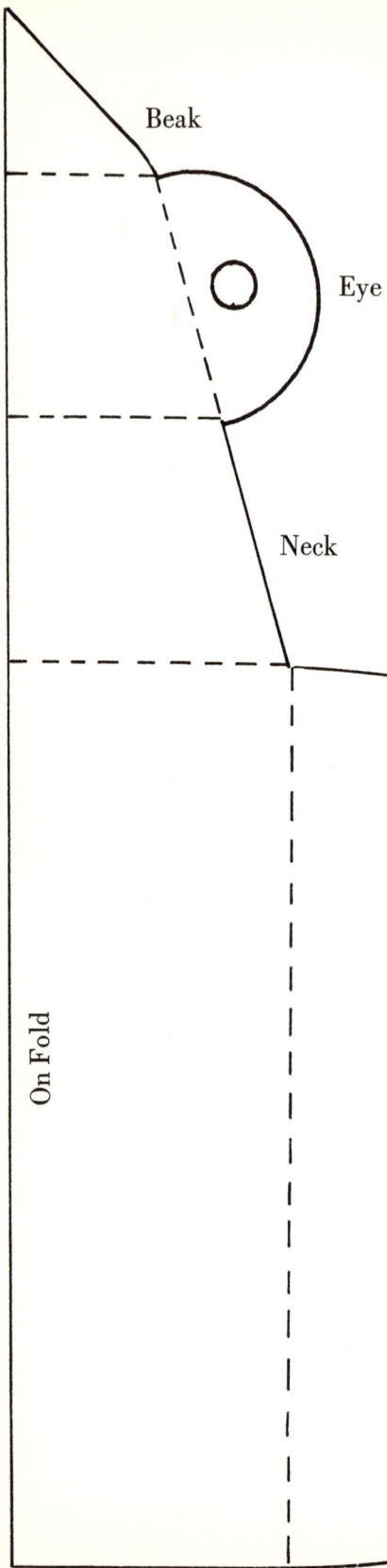

Beak

Eye

Figure 2

Wattle and Eye Lining
Cut two for each eye.
Score and fold on dotted line.

Neck

Figure 1

Hen
Trace and cut out.
Score and fold
dotted lines.

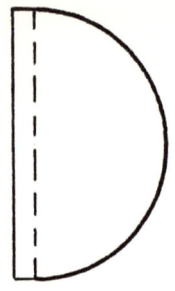

On Fold

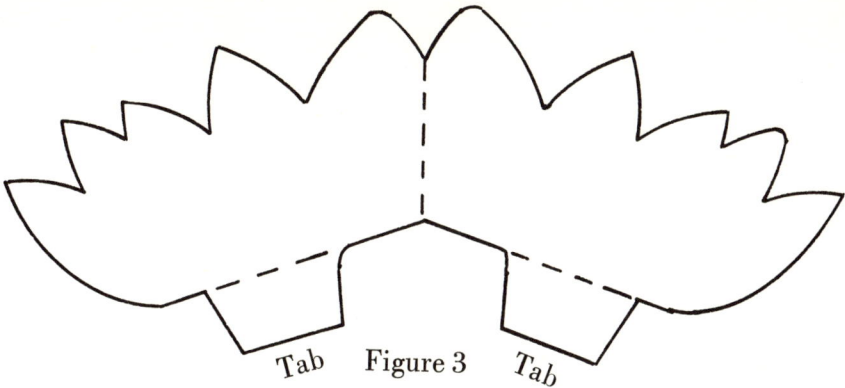

Tab   Figure 3   Tab

Hen's Crest

Trace and cut out.
Fold dotted lines.

Cut dotted lines.

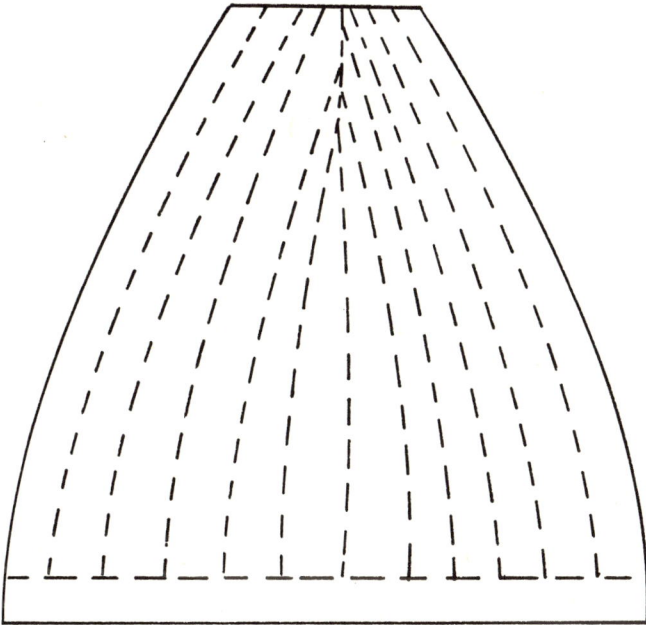

Figure 4

Hen's Tail

Trace and cut out.

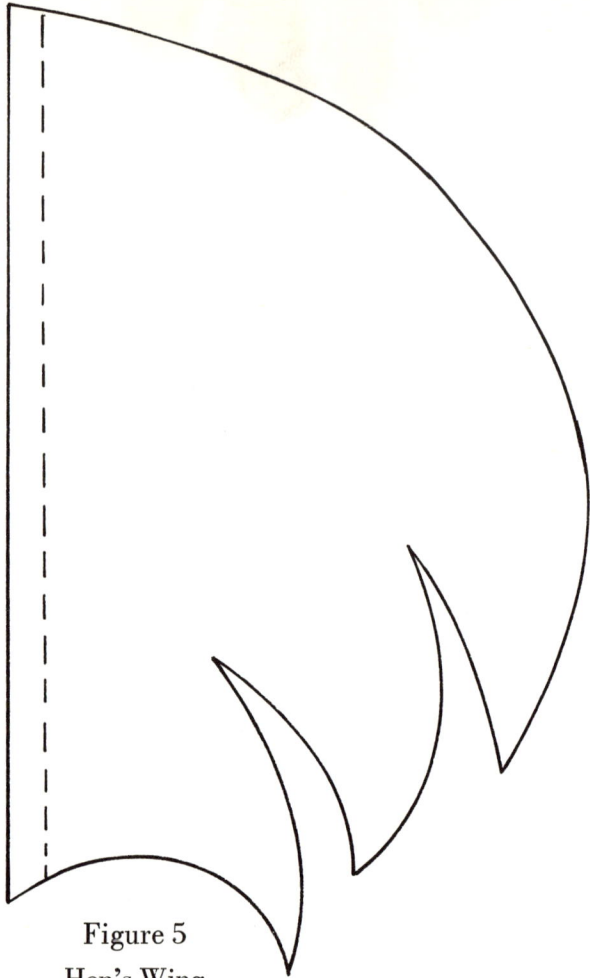

Figure 5
Hen's Wing
Trace and cut out.
Fold dotted line.

2. To attach the tail, apply glue to the tab and place it under the body at the appropriate place.
3. Apply glue to the wing tabs and attach one wing on each side of the body.
4. Glue eye linings under the eyes.
5. Cut two circles of black construction paper and glue one over each eye lining.

120

6. Glue the crest to the top of the head, allowing it to stand upright.

7. Glue each wattle under the eye section so that it hangs down.

8. To decorate the tail and body, cut long narrow strips of construction paper of the same color as the wings. Make them pointed at each end. Glue one side and attach each to the tail section and on top of the body. Stagger the strips to make a design, if you like.

9. Repeat this for the head and neck with V-shaped strips for the pinfeathers.

10. Draw legs with a black flair pen under the wings, as illustrated in Figure 6.

11. To make the head-control string, cut a piece of nylon thread, 10 inches long plus the length of the hen's body. Glue one end of the string under the hen's beak. The control string is pulled back and forth from *under* the hen's body.

Holding the Hen Push-Puppet for Action:

1. Cut a piece of wood about $2\frac{1}{4}$ inches wide and 10 inches long. If you cannot saw wood, ask someone to help you.

2. Stand the hen upright on the wooden base, facing the narrow end, as shown in Figure 6. Allow space in front so that you can place a small nest on it.

3. Fasten the legs to the wood with glue. Allow to dry.

4. To place the hen on stage, push the free end of the wooden base through the back opening.

5. While the actor speaks, pull the head-control string back and forth with one hand. This will make the hen nod. With your other hand, push the free end of the wooden base back and forth just a trifle.

Nest:

A nest can be made by using straw or colored cellophane pa-

121

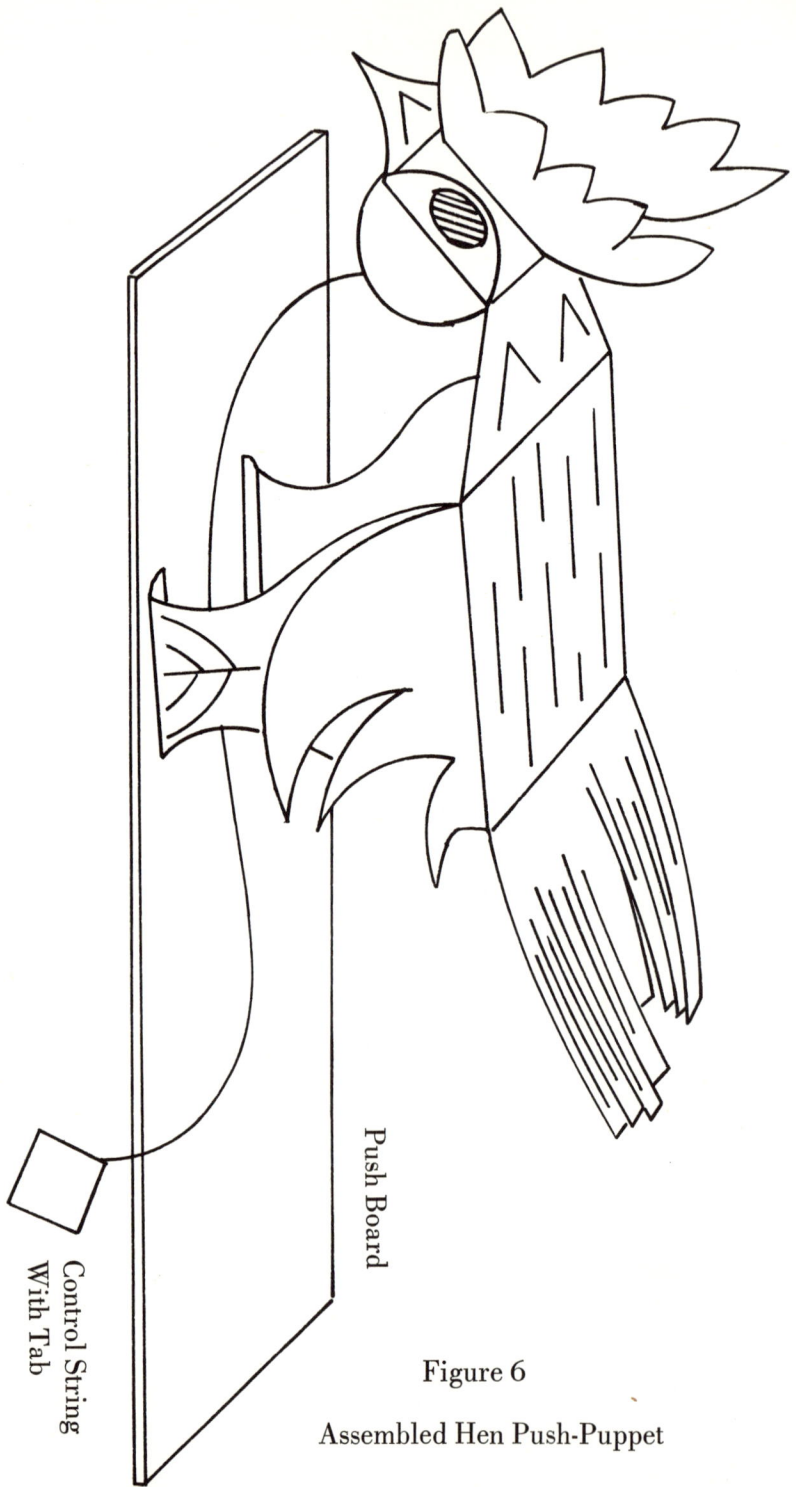

Push Board

Control String
With Tab

Figure 6

Assembled Hen Push-Puppet

per. Shape some into a round form, and firmly press it down in the middle. Narrow strips of newspaper can also be used.

Goose Push-Puppet

Materials:

white Bristol paper, or any rigid construction paper, for body
orange or yellow Bristol paper, or any rigid paper for beak,
    wings, and legs
white thread
round toothpick
scissors
tracing paper
pencil
ruler
Elmer's Glue-All
wooden board, about $2\frac{1}{2}$ by 10 inches

Directions:

BODY:

1. Measure and cut a $12\frac{1}{2}$ by $6\frac{1}{2}$ inch strip of white Bristol paper.

2. Roll it into a wide cone (see Basic Shapes). Make this cone with a very wide base opening by overlapping very slightly.

3. After overlapping the ends of the cone place paper clips at top and bottom overlapping ends to hold them in place.

4. Remove one clip at a time and apply glue to the inner edge. Press to hold. Allow to dry.

5. Do not cut off the triangular excess at the base of the cone.

6. With scissors, slash the triangular segment into narrow strips up to the base of the cone. This becomes the tail. Since the goose has a very narrow tail, trim off any excess, as shown in Figure 1.

123

NECK:

1. Measure and cut a strip of white Bristol paper, 5¼ by 4¼ inches.

2. Roll it into a cylinder. Make it narrow enough to fit snugly into the narrow opening of the body cone.

3. At one end, cut a U-shaped groove.

4. Fit this end into the narrow opening of the body cone, with the groove resting against the bottom of the neck opening.

5. With a pencil make a dot at one side of the cone neck-opening.

6. With a sharp tool—the point of manicure scissors will do—make a small hole through the cone and neck cylinder.

7. Press the point of a round toothpick straight through the cone and neck cylinder and into the opposite side of the neck cylinder.

8. Make a small hole on the opposite side of the cone, which has been slightly marked by the point of the toothpick. Make the hole through the cone and neck cylinder.

9. Press the toothpick point that is in the neck cylinder through the opposite side of the neck cylinder and cone. The neck is now attached to the body with a straight axle hinge. This hinge will allow the neck to move up and down. Dab glue to each end of toothpick to prevent it from slipping through the openings.

10. To move the neck, cut a piece of thread. If a push-board will be used, the thread should be the full length of the goose plus the length of the board. If the goose will be a hand puppet, the thread should be the length of the goose only. Glue one end of the thread to the top of the neck cylinder. Cover it by gluing a small piece of Bristol paper over it. Cut two small pieces of Bristol paper. Glue the other end of the string between these tabs. Allow to dry. This end is pulled back and forth to make the neck nod up and down.

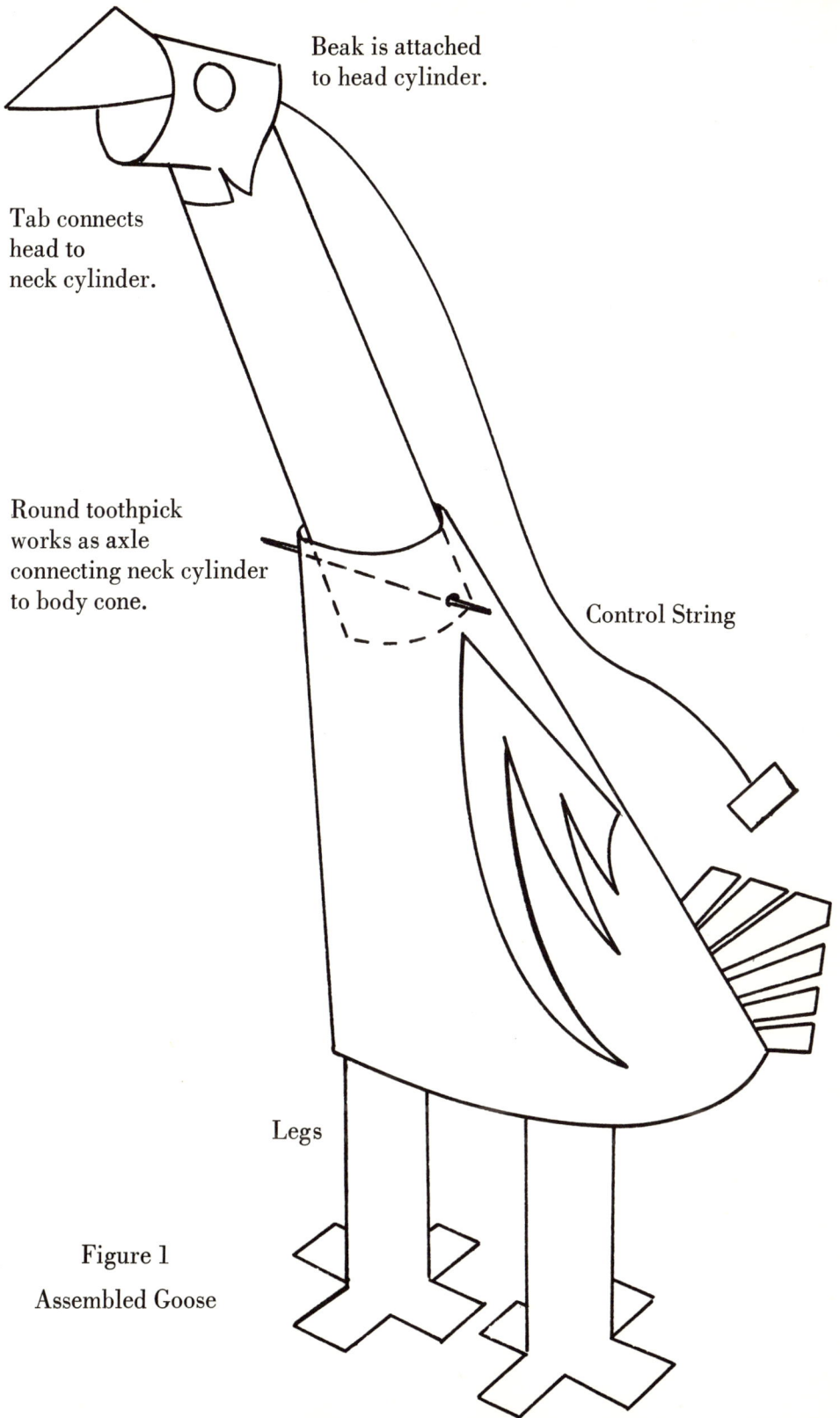

Beak is attached
to head cylinder.

Tab connects
head to
neck cylinder.

Round toothpick
works as axle
connecting neck cylinder
to body cone.

Control String

Legs

Figure 1
Assembled Goose

HEAD:

1. Measure and cut a 5 by 1¾ inch strip of white Bristol paper.

2. Roll it into a cylinder. Glue edges in place and allow to dry.

3. To make the beak, trace Figure 1 to make a pattern. Then transfer the pattern to orange or yellow Bristol paper. Score and bend all dotted lines, as shown in Figure 1 (see Paper Techniques).

4. Overlap the beak as shown in Figure 2 and glue the two sides together. Apply glue on tabs, as shown.

5. Position beak with the tabs on the upper inside of the head cylinder. Press it to hold and allow to dry.

6. With scissors, cut a tab about 1 inch wide and ½ inch deep at the bottom of the head cylinder.

7. Apply glue to the inner side of tab. Position the head at an angle against the upper neck cylinder, so that the head points slightly down. Hold and allow to dry.

8. Cut out two circles of black construction paper, about ½ inch in diameter. Glue one to each side of head, where the eyes should be and allow to dry.

WINGS:

1. Trace Figure 3 to make the wing pattern. Transfer to orange or yellow Bristol paper. Make two wings. Score and bend dotted lines for tabs, as directed.

2. Apply glue to each tab. Position one wing at a slant against body cone on one side of the goose. Hold in place, and allow to dry.

3. Repeat this step for the other wing.

LEGS:

1. Measure and cut out two pieces of orange or yellow Bristol paper, 3 by 3¾ inches. Roll each into a narrow, sturdy cylinder. Glue the ends together.

Figure 2
Goose's Beak
Trace and cut out.
Bend dotted lines.

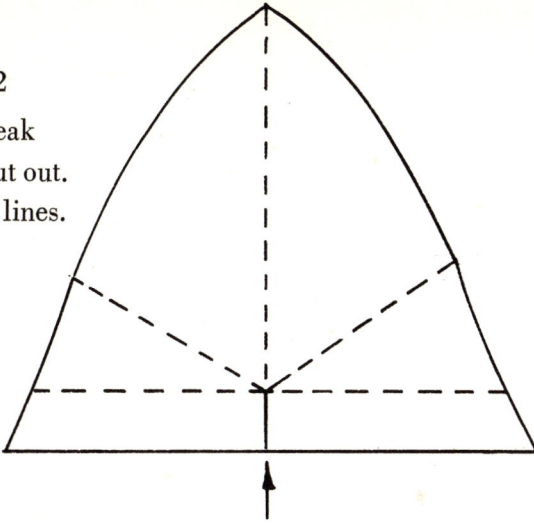

Slash, glue, and attach tabs to head cylinder.

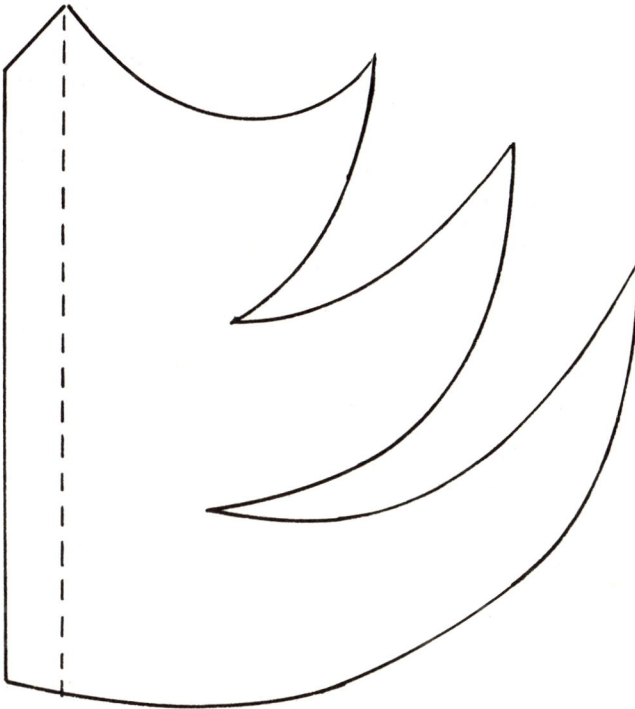

Figure 3
Goose's Wing
Trace and cut out.
Fold dotted line.

127

2. With scissors, cut four slashes around one end of each cylinder. Open the ends of the cylinder to make four tabs that can be glued to a baseboard.

3. To attach the leg to the body, apply glue on one side of the uncut end. Position it against the front inner side of the body cone at the appropriate place. Press to hold. Allow to dry.

4. Do the same with the other leg. Be sure both legs are the same length, so that when it is upright, the goose will be balanced on the board. The assembled goose should look like Figure 1.

Holding Goose Push-Puppet for Action:
1. Cut a 2½ by 10 inch piece of wood.
2. Glue the goose upright on the wooden base, with its head facing the 2½ inch side. Allow space in front for a small nest.
3. This goose can also be held as a hand puppet. To do so, insert one hand through the bottom opening. When the actor speaks, pull the hand-control string up and down with the other hand. The goose will then nod its head.

Rabbit Push-Puppet

Materials:
white Bristol paper or any rigid construction paper
colored gift-wrap paper or colored crayons
white absorbent cotton
black construction paper
white thread
Elmer's Glue-All
scissors
tracing paper
pencil
ruler
wooden board, about 2½ by 10 inches

Directions:

BODY:

1. Trace Figures 1 to 5 to make patterns for the body, haunch, arm, ear, and vest (see Tracing Directions). Transfer all of the patterns, except the vest, to white Bristol paper. Use colored gift-wrap paper for the vest, or color white paper with crayons. Cut all solid lines. Score and bend the dotted lines (see Paper Techniques).

2. Roll the body section into a cone that is partially open in front. Overlap the bottom of the cone as much as necessary, but leave an opening that is large enough to put your hand through. Dab glue on the overlap. Press to hold. Allow to dry.

3. Glue the two flaps at each side of the head, as illustrated, to give the head a three-dimensional look.

4. Bend the rabbit's head so that it overlaps the top of the cone. It will now move up and down over the top of the cone.

5. To attach the vest, dab glue to the neckline and down both sides of the rabbit's body. The open sides are the back of the vest. Slip it over front of body, with its front facing you and the open sides at the back of cone. Attach it as far up and around the cone as it will fit. The vest now covers the front opening of the cone.

6. To attach rabbit's haunches, fold down the tabs, glue one side of each tab, and attach one to each side of body at the appropriate place. Be sure to position hunches so that they will rest on the table when rabbit is placed on the table.

7. Glue on the rabbit's arms, positioning them so that the paws meet in front.

8. To attach rabbit's ears, fold down the tabs and dab glue to front of each tab. Position each ear at a corner of rabbit's head, so that half of the tab is attached to the back of the head and the other half to the side of the head. Press to hold. Allow to dry.

129

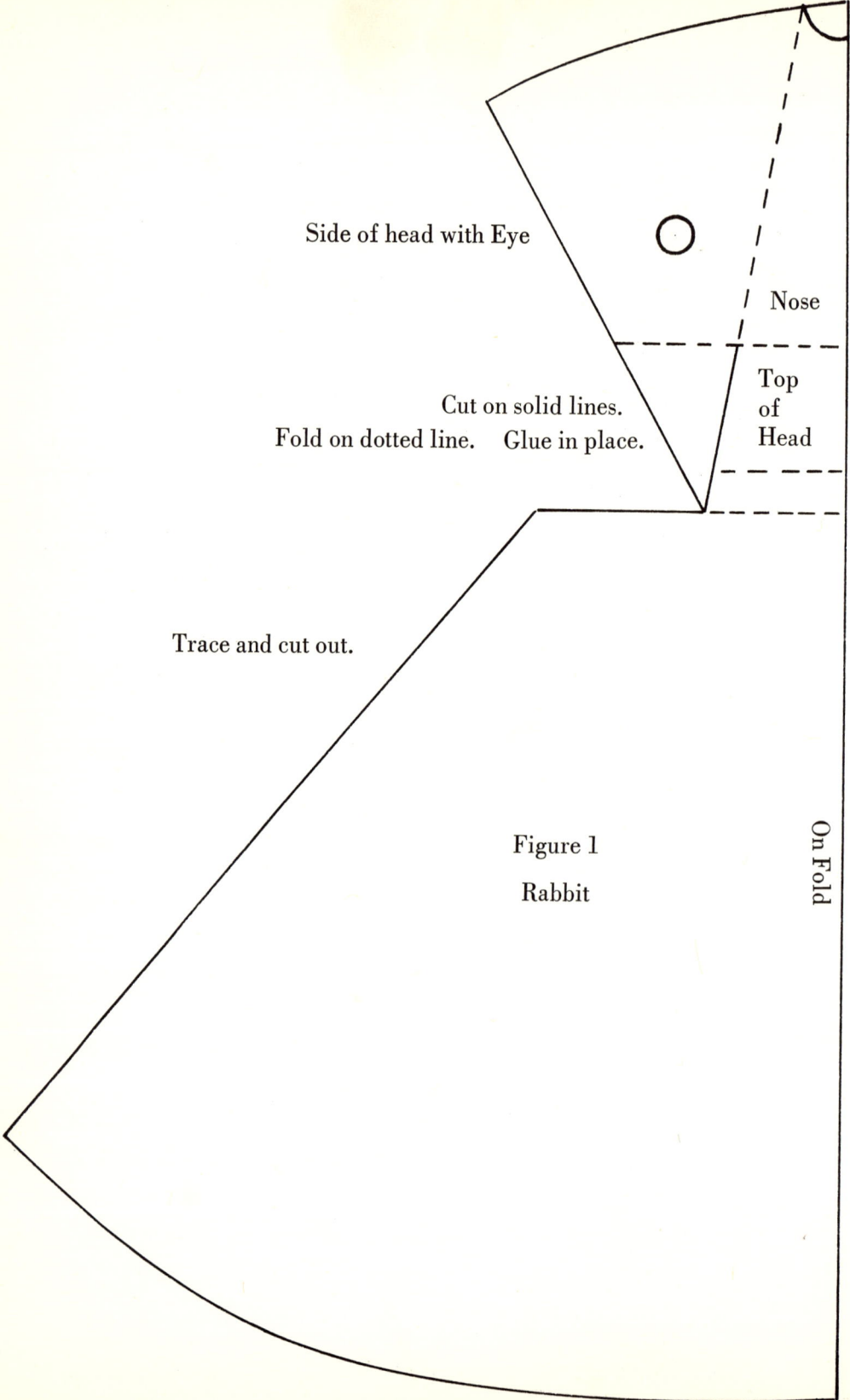

Side of head with Eye

Nose

Cut on solid lines.
Fold on dotted line.   Glue in place.

Top
of
Head

Trace and cut out.

Figure 1

Rabbit

On Fold

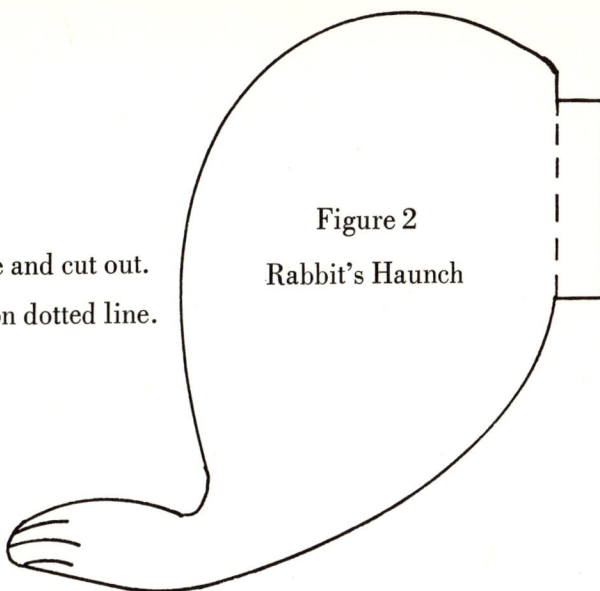

Trace and cut out.

Fold on dotted line.

Figure 2

Rabbit's Haunch

Draw lines for toes.

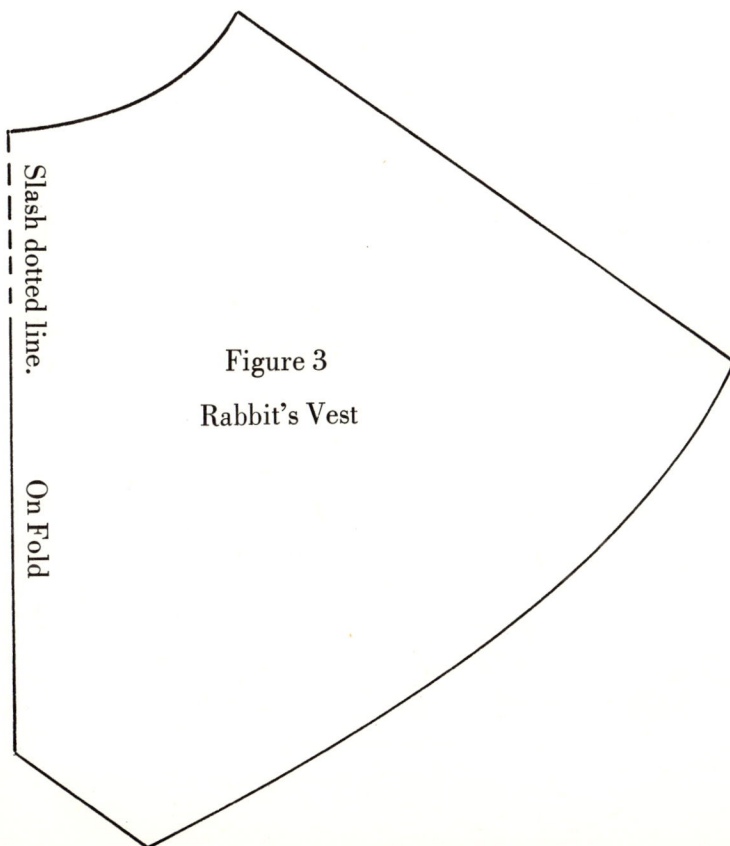

Slash dotted line.

On Fold

Figure 3

Rabbit's Vest

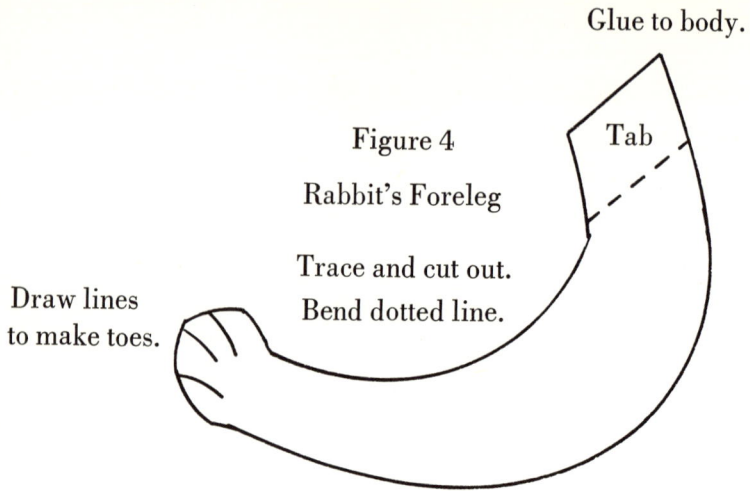

Glue to body.

Figure 4

Rabbit's Foreleg

Tab

Draw lines
to make toes.

Trace and cut out.
Bend dotted line.

Figure 5

Rabbit's Ear

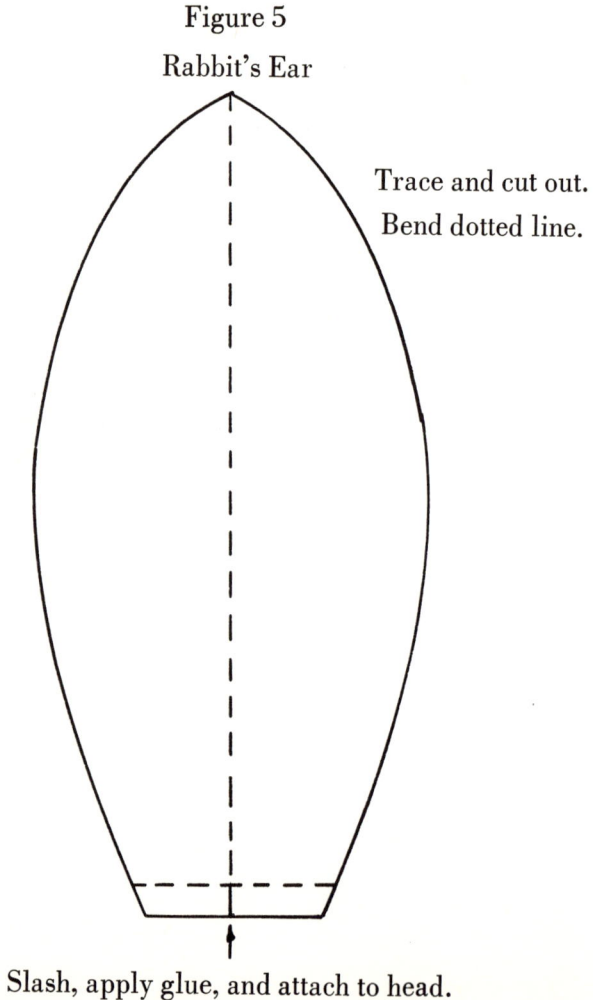

Trace and cut out.

Bend dotted line.

Slash, apply glue, and attach to head.

9. For the tail, dab glue to a piece of round white absorbent cotton. Attach it to the back of cone at appropriate place. Press to hold. Allow to dry.

10. Cut two ½ inch diameter circles out of black construction paper for eyes. Glue one to each side of the head.

11. Cut a semicircular piece of black construction paper to make a nose, and glue it on. Press to hold. Allow to dry.

12. To move the head, cut a piece of thread. If a push-board will be used to move the puppet, the thread should be the full length of the board. If the rabbit is to be used as a hand puppet, the thread should be the full length of the rabbit only. Glue one end under the rabbit's nose, out of sight. Secure it by gluing a small piece of construction paper over it. The other end of thread is inserted through the top of the cone opening to the bottom of the cone. Glue this end of thread between two small pieces of construction paper, to be used as holding tabs. Pull the control string back and forth to make the rabbit's head nod up and down.

BASKET:

1. Draw and cut out a circle, 3½ inches in diameter, using construction paper of any color. Cut the circle in half.

2. Form a cone from half of the circle and staple or glue the edges together.

3. Cut a ¾ by 4 inch strip from the same construction paper. Staple or glue each end to the inner opening of the cone.

4. Hang the basket over the rabbit's paws and staple or glue it in place.

5. Fill the basket with pieces of colored paper to represent cane and berries. Later, fill it with jelly beans.

133

Holding the Rabbit for Action:

1. Glue the rabbit to the 2½ by 10 inch piece of wood, facing the narrow end. Make sure that the rim of the cone sticks to the wood.

2. To place the rabbit on stage, push the wooden base through the back opening.

3. This rabbit can be held as a hand puppet. Insert your hand through the bottom opening.

4. When the actor speaks, pull the control string up and down with the other hand. The rabbit will then nod his head.

Turkey Push-Puppet

Materials:
poster board, yellow
construction paper, orange, green, brown, red
Elmer's Glue-All
scissors
pencil
ruler
stapler and staples
wooden board, about 3½ by 10 inches

Directions:
BODY:

1. Construct a cylinder from a 3½ by 15 inch strip of yellow poster board (see Basic Shapes). Staple edges together. This will make a 5 inch cylinder.

134

2. To close the back opening of the body cylinder, make a circle, 5½ inches in diameter, from a piece of yellow construction paper. Make ½ inch slashes around the circle's edge. These will be tabs. Bend and apply glue under each tab. Position the circle to the back of the cylinder. Press each tab against side of cylinder, all the way around. Allow to dry.

NECK:

1. Make a 6 inch high cone of yellow construction paper.

2. Make several ½ inch slashes around top and bottom openings. These are tabs.

3. Bend the tabs at the base of the cone, and apply glue under each.

4. Position neck cone against the top of body cylinder. Overlap the front tabs of the neck over top front of body cylinder. Tabs that do not touch the body cylinder may be turned under. Press all tabs against the body cylinder. Hold until dry.

HEAD:

1. Make a 4 inch high cone of yellow construction paper.

2. Bend back the tabs at the top of the neck cone. Apply glue under each tab.

3. Position head cone, with the narrow end facing forward at the top of the neck, so that the tabs will overlap it. Press to hold.

4. Allow to dry.

CHEST:

1. Draw and cut out three circles; the first, 6 inches in diameter, of brown construction paper; another, 5 inches in diameter, of green construction paper; and another, 4 inches in diameter, of orange construction paper.

135

2. Cut V-shaped notches around each circle, about ½ inch deep, as illustrated in Figure 1.

Draw and cut out
three sizes and colors.

Glue one over the other.

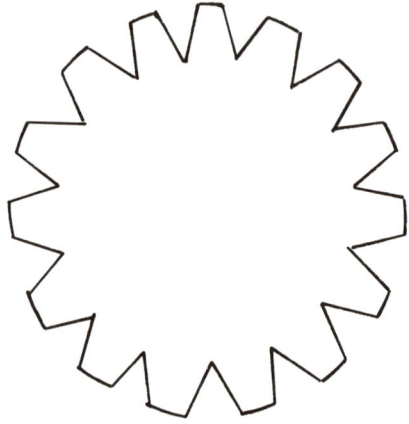

Figure 1

Turkey Chest Covering

3. Apply glue around back of the 6 inch circle, where it will be attached to the front edge of body cylinder. Cover the front opening of the body cylinder with it. Press to hold. Allow to dry.

4. Glue and superimpose the 5 inch circle over the 6 inch circle. Allow to dry.

5. Glue the 4 inch circle over the 5 inch circle. Allow to dry.

TAIL:

1. Cut out orange construction paper, 18 by 6 inches. Cut V-shaped notches along one 18 inch side, about 1 inch deep.

2. Pleat it into a fan (see Paper Techniques).

3. Gather pleats along the unnotched side, and apply glue to one surface of the edge. Also apply a dab of glue to lower portion of first and last pleat on the same surface.

4. Spread the glued side against turkey's back cylinder as far

136

as it will go to fan out gracefully. Press pleated edges against cylinder, with first and last pleats glued firmly against the body cylinder. Hold firmly with fingers until dry.

5. If you like, cut small pieces of construction paper from another color, and glue one on each pleat to decorate it.

WINGS:

1. Follow steps 1 and 2 for making the tail, using a 9 by 5 inch piece of orange construction paper.

2. Staple the pleats on the unnotched edge together, excluding the first and last pleat. This becomes the top side of the wing, with the middle pleats held together.

3. Apply glue under the bottoms of the first and last pleats of the unnotched edges and also along top edge of the stapled pleats.

4. Attach the wing to the side of the body cylinder, with the notched edges downward. The glued portions of the first and last pleats are pressed firmly against cylinder to hold. Allow to dry.

5. Do the same with second wing on the opposite side of the body cylinder.

6. Decorate the same as the tail, if you like.

WATTLE:

1. Follow Steps 1 and 2 for making the tail, using a $3\frac{1}{2}$ by 6 inch piece of red construction paper. Cut notches at one narrow edge.

2. Gather pleats at the unnotched edge. Apply glue between each pleat, at top, to hold. Allow to dry.

3. Cut a small curve at this end. Apply glue to the underside. Slip it under turkey's head at the front top part of the neck cone, like a long bib. Press to hold. Allow to dry.

4. Cut a narrow strip of the same red construction paper.

Apply glue to one side and wind it around the front part of head cone several times. Allow one end to hang over. This is part of turkey's wattle.

CROWN:

1. Cut out green construction paper, $2\frac{1}{2}$ inches by 1 inch. Fold 1 inch side in half. Now you have a folded strip that is $2\frac{1}{2}$ inches by $\frac{1}{2}$ inch. Cut $\frac{1}{2}$ inch slits up to the fold.

2. Apply glue to the solid section of the strip and wrap it around wide opening of turkey's head.

EYES:

1. Cut out two small disks from black construction paper, and two smaller yellow disks. Glue the yellow disks on the black disks. Glue black disks on each side of the turkey's head.

LEGS:

1. Cut out a piece of rigid yellow construction paper, 2 by 2 inches. Make a cylinder.

2. Cut about four or five slits at both ends of the cylinder, about $\frac{1}{2}$ inch. Bend and open tabs at both ends.

3. Apply glue to the inner sides of the tabs at one end of the cylinder. Position against the bottom of the body cylinder at the appropriate place. Press to hold. Allow to dry.

4. Do the same with second leg. Be sure both cylinders are equal in length, so that they will hold the turkey's body straight when it is standing upright on base of table. The completed turkey should look like Figure 2.

Holding Push-Puppet for Action:

1. Apply glue to bottom of tabs.

2. Position turkey at the front end of the wooden board so that both legs are balanced on the width of board. Leave space in front for a small nest. Press to hold. Allow to dry.

3. To place the turkey on stage, push the wooden base through the back opening.

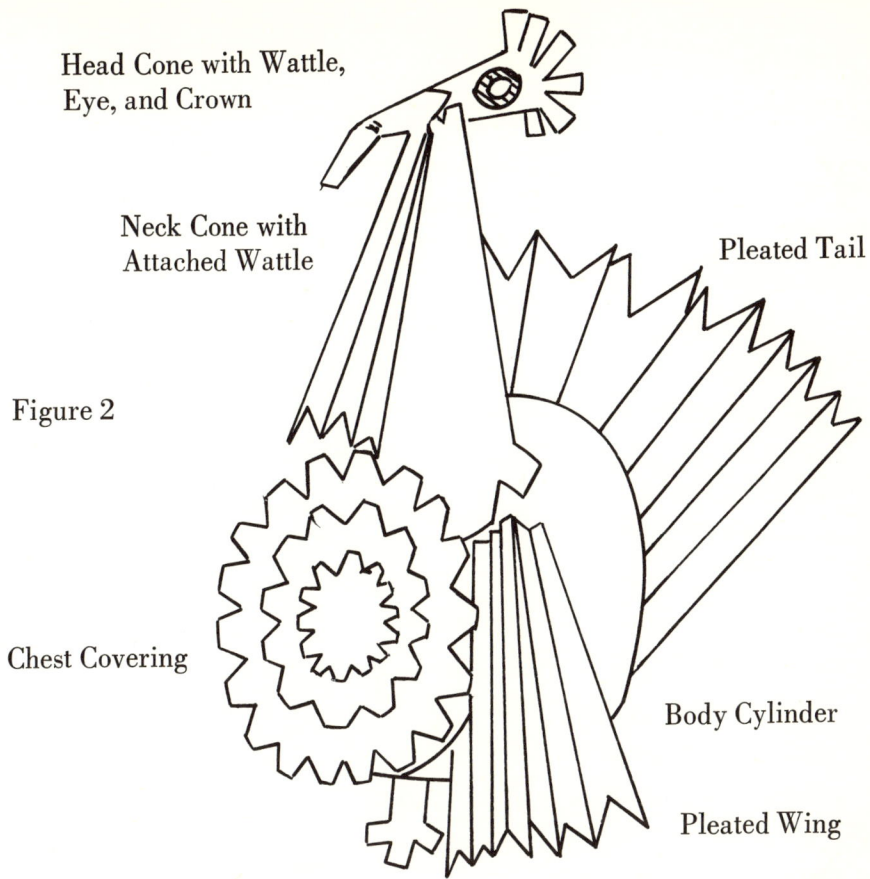

Head Cone with Wattle, Eye, and Crown

Neck Cone with Attached Wattle

Pleated Tail

Figure 2

Chest Covering

Body Cylinder

Pleated Wing

Herald Push-Puppet

Materials:
railroad board, color of your choice
construction paper, two colors of your choice
two Q-tips
flair pen, black and red
stapler and staples
Elmer's Glue-All
scissors

139

pencil

tracing paper

ruler

Directions:

BODY:

1. Trace Figures 1 and 2 to make patterns and transfer to railroad board. Cut solid lines, score and bend dotted lines as illustrated (see Paper Techniques).

2. Attach top half of body to lower half with Scotch tape, or glue the two halves together by overlapping one over the other, about ½ inch.

3. Draw the nose and mouth with a red flair pen; draw eyes and a mustache with a black flair pen.

4. For trouser stripes, cut out two narrow strips of black construction paper, and glue one down the center of each trouser.

5. To make the hat cover, trace Figures 3, 4, and 5 to make patterns. Transfer Figures 3 and 4 to railroad board of any color, and Figure 5 to black construction paper. If possible, glue a soft feather to Figure 5. Glue the hat decoration to the center of the hat cover so that part of it will stand upright above the top.

6. Glue the decorated hat cover over the hat on the figure. Press to hold. Allow to dry.

7. Fold trousers on the dotted line, with the stripes outward. Fold, overlap, and glue together the two flaps at the bottom of the trousers. The figure will stand on the base when it is glued to it.

ARMS:

1. Make cat-stairs with two 18 by ¾ inch strips of colored construction paper (see Paper Techniques).

2. Staple or glue one end to the herald's shoulder.

3. Repeat Steps 1 and 2 to make the second arm.

Trouser
Stripes

Figure 2

Trousers

Trace and cut out.

Figure 1

Standing
Base

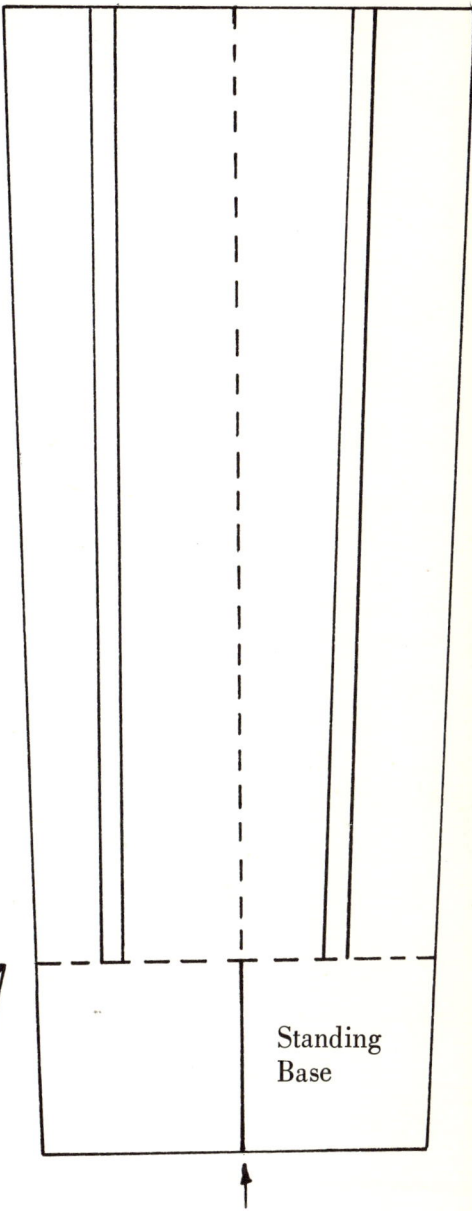

Slash, glue, and
fold under to form a square.

Trace and cut out.

Figure 3

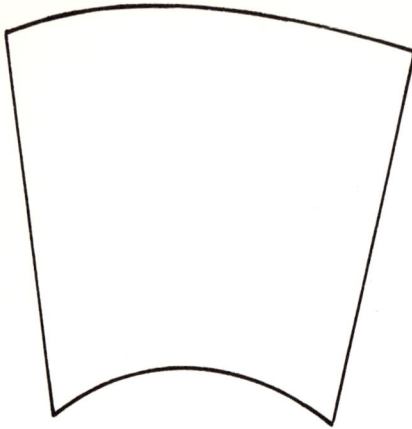

Hat Cover and Visor
Trace and cut out

Figure 4

Figure 5
Hat Decoration
Trace and cut out.

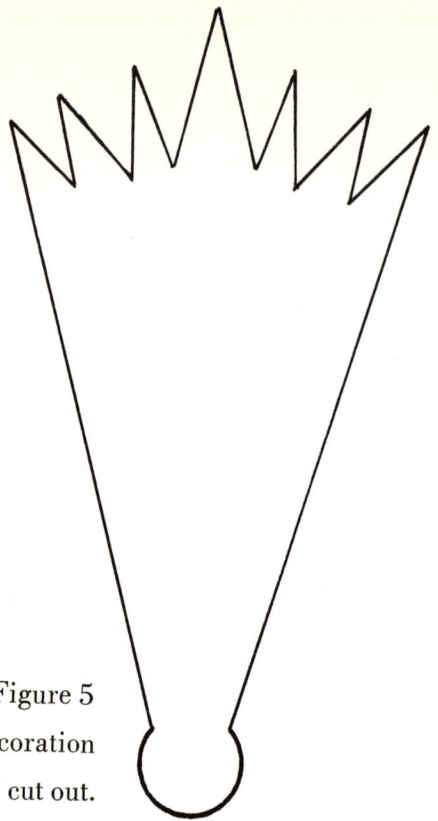

DRUM:

1. Using railroad board, draw a 3 inch diameter circle.

2. Around this circle, draw a 4 inch diameter circle. You have one circle within another, or two concentric circles.

3. Cut around the outer circle only.

4. Draw four tabs between the outer and inner circles. Cut the outer circle away from the four tabs, as shown in Figure 6. The 3 inch circle now has four tabs.

5. Score and bend each tab along the dotted lines, as shown.

6. Make a second circle, following Steps 1 to 4.

7. Measure and cut a strip of railroad board of another color, 11 by 1¾ inches.

8. With a black flair pen, decorate the strip with large crosses, as shown in Figure 7.

142

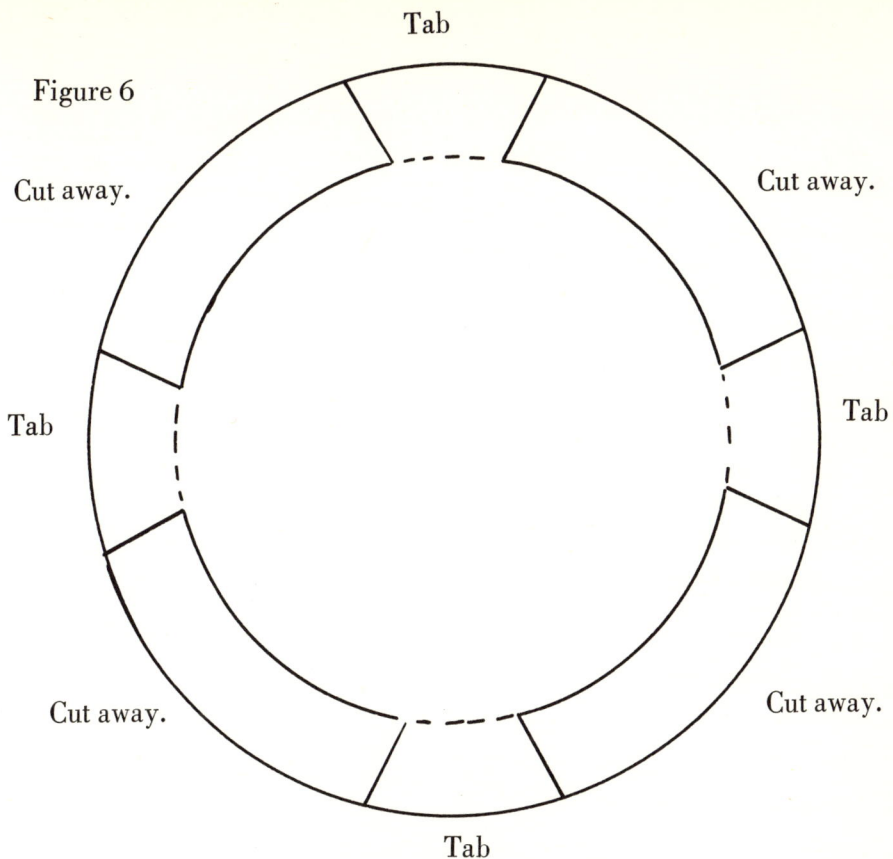

Figure 6

Tab

Cut away.

Cut away.

Tab

Tab

Cut away.

Cut away.

Tab

Side of Herald's Drum

Cut two.

Score and bend dotted lines.

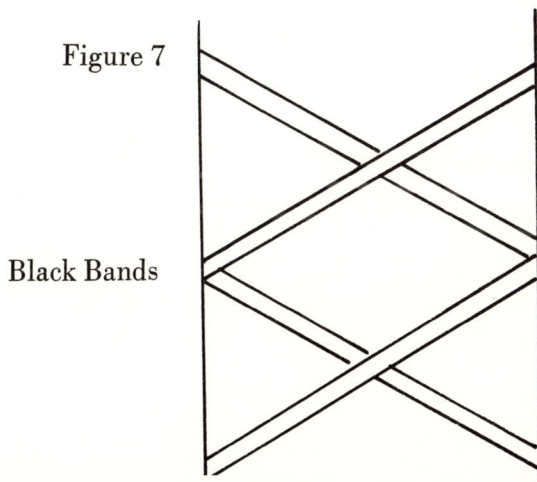

Figure 7

Black Bands

Drum Strip, 11″ x 1¾″

9. Pull the strip over the edge of a table or desk to curve it.

10. Dab glue to the tabs of one circle, and attach them to the strip. Press to hold. Allow to dry. Work one tab at a time until all four tabs are glued to the strip.

11. Do the same with the second circle.

12. Overlap and glue excess strip. Now you have a snugly fitted drum.

13. Apply a dab of glue to the side of the drum and position it against the front of the figure so that about 1 inch of herald's legs are seen beneath it. Press to hold. Allow to dry.

14. Remove cotton from one end of a Q-tip. Apply glue to this end of the Q-tip. Position it diagonally between the last square on the herald's arm so that the hammer of the drumstick points toward the drum. Press to hold. Allow to dry.

15. Do the same with the second drumstick. If you do not have Q-tips, use round toothpicks with a bit of absorbent cotton glued to one end of each.

Now the Herald can beat his drum when he is shaken from side to side.

Holding the Puppet for Action:

1. Glue the herald upright and on the front end of a $2\frac{1}{2}$ by 10 inch piece of wood.

2. To place the push-puppet on stage, push the free end of the wooden base through the back opening.

3. The cat-stair arms are flexible and should shake so that the herald looks as though he is beating his drum when the pushboard is shaken from side to side.

Bird Rod Puppet

Materials:
one piece of standard bond typing paper
white thread

narrow rod, about 15 inches long

scissors

stapler and staples

ruler

pencil

Elmer's Glue-All

Directions:

1. Measure and cut two strips of typing paper, 1¾ by 11 inches.

2. To make a beak, staple or glue the two strips together at one end.

3. Loop the upper strip over the lower strip and staple or glue them together to shape the head.

4. Overlap the other two ends of the strips and staple or glue them together to make the body.

5. To make head feathers, cut three strips of typing paper, ¾ inch wide and of various lengths. Curl each strip with a scissor blade or a knife (see Paper Techniques).

6. Staple together the straight ends of curled strips, one on top of the other. Be sure the curled ends fall gracefully over one another. Apply glue to the bottom of the stapled end. Attach the strips to the top of the head. Press to hold. Allow to dry.

7. Measure and cut strips of typing paper, 5 by 4 inches to make the tail. Cut the 4 inch sides, making slashes about ¾ of an inch apart up to about ½ inch from the opposite ends. This will give you several slashed strips.

8. Curl each strip individually with a scissor blade or a knife.

9. Make cylinder by overlapping the sides about ¾ inch. Be sure the paper strips curl outwardly. These become the bird's feathered tail.

10. Cut a few darts here and there on the straight edge. These become tabs.

145

11. Apply glue to bottom of each tab, and glue the tabs to the bird's body at the back. Press to hold. Allow to dry.

Now you have an abstract bird.

Suggestions for Making Other Types of Birds:
Birds can be made in many different ways. They can be drawn and cut from a piece of flat construction paper, with wings and tail pleated like fans and attached. They can also be constructed with paper cones and cylinders. Another way, is to draw and cut them out on the fold of a piece of construction paper, giving you two sides that are exactly alike.

Holding the Puppet for Action:
1. Measure and cut a piece of white thread, 10 inches long.
2. Glue one end to the top and center of bird's body. Finding the point at which to place this should not be difficult. Stick a straight pin in the back at a point that seems to be the point of balance. If the bird tips forward or back, then the pinhole must be adjusted before gluing the thread to its back.
3. Cut a piece of typing paper small enough to cover the glued thread. Press to hold. Allow to dry.
4. Attach the other end of the thread to the top of the narrow rod by winding it around several times and knotting. Apply glue. Allow to dry.
5. Hold the free end of the rod in your hand. As the actor speaks, move the rod slightly. The bird will swing and sway.

Production Notes

Scenery and Properties:
A barnyard scene is painted on the backdrop, with a large red barn surrounded by trees and perhaps a few garden tools.

Trees are fastened to the floor of the puppet stage.

146

At first, the rabbit carries a basket filled with colored pieces of construction paper to represent the sugar cane and berry juice he has for sale. Later, the basket is filled with colored jelly beans.

Make a nest from straw cellophane paper or shredded newspaper for each barnyard character. Fill them with eggs made of small pieces of white crumpled construction paper. The king carries a small bag of gold at the end.

Action:
When needed, place a nest of eggs on the board in front of each barnyard animal. If hand puppets are used instead of the

push-puppets, place the nest on the floor in front of the puppet.

The climax of this play is the spilling of the eggs from the nests, when the characters shove and push one another. During this scene, push the puppets vigorously, and be sure to upset the nests. The rest of the action is described in the play.

A good-sized stage is recommended for this puppet show, since several characters appear at one time.

148

COLUMBUS DAY

The Admiral and
the Feathered Pilots

LAURA ROSS

Characters:

Christopher Columbus, Admiral of the *Niña,* the *Pinta,* and the *Santa Maria*

Juan De La Cosa, master of the Santa Maria

Rodrigo, seaman

Bartolme, seaman

several birds

several sailors in the background

Narrator (*speaks from behind a closed curtain*): How the *Niña, Pinta,* and *Santa Maria* sailed that first week in October, 1492. Admiral Christopher Columbus had promised his men they would sight land by sailing west. After thirty days at sea with no sight of land, there were rumblings of revolt among his sailors.

At Curtain Rise:

It is nighttime, and stage is in semidarkness. Rodrigo and Bartolme stand on the deck of the *Santa Maria.* A railing marks

149

the edge of the deck, and we see part of a tall mast with rigging.

Rodrigo (*disgusted*): It's been over thirty days since we loaded our ships with stores, water, and firewood, and anchors were raised. In all this time, there has been no sight of land!

Bartolme (*angrily*): If we follow this westerly course much longer, it will be our ruin.

Rodrigo: Food and water will give out, for it never rains in this desert waste of salt water.

Bartolme (*in lowered tone*): After all, Columbus is a foreigner. Wouldn't it be a good plan to heave him overboard, and to pretend that when observing the stars he had fallen in by accident?

Rodrigo (*excited*): We'll do it. It's the only means for our safe return. (*Both exit.*)

Columbus (*enters after a short while, accompanied by Juan*): Have you ever seen such a night for sailing, Juan?

Juan (*looking skyward*): The stars are so low you could almost touch them.

Columbus (*looking seaward*): And look at the waves. They move so gently—almost as though the ocean were breathing.

Juan (*looking seaward*): The seaweeds are so thick around us. What if they were to ensnare the ship and pull it down?

Columbus: Nonsense, Juan. The sea is full of life, but nothing that could harm us.

Juan: It is said that the sea holds horrible monsters that will reach up and drag our ships down.

Columbus: Juan, you are an intelligent man. Do you believe that?

Juan: No, my Captain. (*A group of sailors appear to be con-*

versing in the background.) But the men on board are fearful, so much so, that they're beginning to talk mutiny. They want you to turn the ships back to Spain. Some are talking about stabbing you in the back and throwing you overboard if you don't turn the ships back. They fear that soon we will sail to the edge of the sea and that monsters will reach up and drag us down to the bottomless pit. (*Moans are heard in the background. Rodrigo and Bartolme enter stealthily.*)

Columbus (*alerted*): Who goes there?

Rodrigo: It is only your sailors, Captain Columbus.

Columbus: Why are you wandering about when you should be sleeping?

Bartolme: We're afraid to sleep, Captain Columbus.

Rodrigo: Before long, we will be entrapped in this mass of seaweed that spreads thick around our ship.

Bartolme: It is a trap. Soon the monsters and dragons will reach up and pull our ship down. (*Moans from the sailors in the background are heard.*)

Columbus: The seaweed you see around is only plant life that lives in the sea. As for monsters, there are no monsters or dragons. Only fish. Fish that are wondrous beyond our imagination. A marvelous natural world exists in the sea, as ours is to us.

Rodrigo: We want to turn back to Spain before it is too late.

Sailors in background: Yes, yes, turn back, turn back!

Columbus: Too late for what?

Rodrigo: Too late to turn back. We'll fall off the edge into a bottomless pit. (*Moans and groans from other sailors are heard in the background.*)

Columbus (*exasperated, but kindly*): Rodrigo, Bartolme, the world is round, not flat. We won't fall off the edge. It is a large world. We don't know how large, but we shall

151

find out. We shall keep sailing due west, and I'm sure we will soon find land.

Juan (*authoritatively*): You heard the Capitan! Now back to your berths, or you will have me to answer to.

Columbus (*pleading*): Give me a few more days—two or three days—and hold to the westerly course. If we do not sight land within that time, we'll turn back.

Rodrigo (*incredulous*): Do we have your word?

Columbus: Yes, I give you my word of honor. (*The sailors exit.*)

Juan (*incredulous*): Captain Columbus, are you serious?

Columbus (*with resignation*): Yes, Juan, I am. The men are good men, but they are tired and discouraged. I have given them my word, and I intend to keep it. (*Columbus paces back and forth. The light gradually becomes brighter as dawn approaches. Eventually there is full light.*)

Juan: Captain, do you hear anything? (*Both listen attentively. Suddenly a sound comes from a distance.*)

Columbus (*excited*): Yes! I hear it! What can it be? (*The sound stops.*) I guess it was only our imaginations, Juan. (*Both pace back and forth for a while. Again the sound is heard but now it is louder, as if it were approaching the ship.*)

Juan (*excited*): There it is again! What can be making such a queer, screeching sound? Can it be the monsters? (*Suddenly a flock of birds is seen flying from one end of the ship to the other.*) Birds! Birds, my Captain! And look! They are flying west by southwest! They're not going in our direction! Surely the birds know what they are doing! They're flying southwesterly, toward their land!

Columbus (*shouts*): Watch belo-o-w! Man your stations and keep a sharp watch. Change course to west by southwest!

Follow the birds! Follow those feathered pilots!

Rodrigo and Bartolme (*there is great excitement as the sailors reappear, straining to see land. Each talks excitedly ad-libbing*): Birds! The birds! Do you think that means land? See! They're showing us the way. (*There is agitation in the background, and we hear shouts.*) Birds! See the birds!

Columbus (*excited*): Men, think of the rewards that are waiting for you ahead. (*He points to the right and the sailors strain to see.*) In India, the roofs of the houses are made of gold! There are mountains and mountains of gold! There are silks and spices. All this will be yours. And think of the glory you will bring to Spain! (*He pauses a moment. The men murmur in excited tones. Then Columbus speaks again, briskly this time.*) Well, what do you say? Shall we turn back?

Sailors (*shouting excitedly*): No! No! Sail on! Sail on, Captain Columbus!

Columbus: Very well! We sail on. On to the west by the southwest! The birds have shown us the way! (*There are joyous shouts in the background as the curtain closes.*)

Christopher Columbus Puppet

This is a free-form puppet made by taking advantage of the natural shape of a piece of scrap wood. Making puppets with scraps of wood can be challenging, since the natural shapes of the wood suggest many forms for characters, both real and unreal. If one studies scrap wood from all sides with an imaginative eye, one can see a person's face, a fish, a bird, a robot, or even an outer-space character. Some wood has interesting grain with textural quality of great beauty. Try rubbing wax into such a piece and then buff it to bring out the natural grain.

Materials:

scrap wood, suggesting and defining a profile with a holding handle, over-all size about 15 inches high, 6 inches at widest part; or stiff cardboard, cut as a free-form profile, same size

cellophane scraps, red, if possible, or any other color; or strips of crepe paper

construction paper, brown, black, blue, red

large feather

Elmer's Glue-All

pencil

scissors

Directions:

1. After selecting a piece of scrap wood that suggests a profile, study it carefully and mark off general areas for the hair, eyes, and mouth. You need not construct a nose, since the scrap of wood should have a natural shape for the nose.

2. To make the hair, glue shreds of red cellophane, or any color, around the top and sides of the scrap wood.

3. Trace Figure 1 to make a pattern for the eyelash (see Tracing Directions). Transfer the pattern to blue or black construction paper, cut it out, and slash the dotted lines.

Figure 1

Eye
Trace and cut out.

Cut dotted lines to make eyelashes.

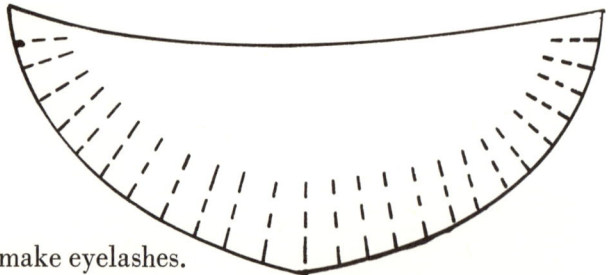

4. Apply glue to both corners of each eyelash, and attach one to each side of the profile. For a three-dimensional effect, allow the center of the eyelid to remain detached from the wood.

5. The pupils can be two 1 inch diameter circles cut from blue construction paper and glued to the wood, under each eyelash.

6. Make the mouth from a strip of red construction paper, about 4 by 2 inches. Fold the 2 inch side in half to form a folded strip, 1 by 4 inches. Apply glue to one side of the strip and attach it to the wood around the edge of the profile under the nose. Be sure the two edges of the strip face forward. These will become the upper and lower lips, as illustrated in Figure 2 and the photograph.

Figure 2

Assembled Columbus

Eyes, lips, hair, hat,
and feather are added.

155

7. To make a hat, draw and cut out a circle of brown construction paper, 7 inches in diameter (see Basic Shapes).
8. Apply glue to the center and attach it, at an angle, to top of the head, over the hair. Press to hold. Allow to dry. Glue a feather to the hat as shown in the photographs, bending the quill if necessary.

Suggestions for Other Puppets in the Play:
The other characters in the play can also be made with scraps of wood, but they would have simpler hats. The hats can be made with the heel ends of discarded nylon stockings, which suggest the shapes of the sailor hats worn at the time. Also, Columbus had red hair; therefore the other characters should have hair of different colors to distinguish one from other.

The birds are rod puppets. See instructions for the bird rod puppet and suggestions for making other types of birds in the Easter project.

A crowd of sailors, may be represented as rod puppets in the background. Cut them out of cardboard, attach them to holding rods, and color them with crayon if you like.

Holding the Puppet for Action:
The wood suggests a profile with a handle tapering down. Hold the puppet by this handle and move it in front of a backdrop in full view of the audience. The puppets can also be used as silhouettes behind a screen.

Production Notes

Scenery and Properties:
On the backdrop is a painting of the ocean, with the Niña and Pinta sailing in it. A wooden rail in the foreground represents the foredeck of the Santa Maria. Part of a wooden mast with rigging is the only other prop needed.

156

Action:

At night a blue light shines on stage. A bright light shines on the stage during the day. To show a group of discontented sailors, use several stick puppets in the background. Actors behind stage mutter and grumble as they move the stick puppets around when the sailors are considering mutiny. Keep stick puppets moving stealthily in the background, with the actors ad-libbing when appropriate. The appearance of the birds is a surprise, but we hear the sound effects before we actually see them.

At the proper time, move the birds from one side of the puppet stage to the other. Three or four would be sufficient if they circle the stage.

HALLOWEEN

The Three Terrors

R O W E N A   B E N N E T T

This play calls for audience participation (a boy and a girl), a technique that was frequently employed in the traditional Italian and French puppet shows.

Characters:
Pumpkin Head
Scarecrow
Witch
Boy
Girl

Properties:
caldron
broomstick
trees

At Curtain Rise:
Pumpkin Head, Scarecrow, and Witch are dancing around a caldron in the center of a field, mumbling and muttering in a kind of chant.

Pumpkin Head:

We are the three, the fearful three

Of whom the world's afraid.

Scarecrow:

There never was a gang so bold

Or bad as our brigade.

Witch:

We are the three, the fearful three

Of whom the world's afraid.

Pumpkin Head (*breaking away from other two and bowing to audience. Witch stirs her caldron mumbling to herself, Scarecrow gestures with his arms*):

I am a pumpkin head called "Jack."

I have a fiery face.

It's lots of fun to see folks run

When I begin to chase.

There's not a boy, there's not a girl,

But runs away from me.

Beware, beware, you'll get a scare.

I'm terrible to see.

Boy's Voice (*from audience*): Ho, ho, ho!

Girl's Voice (*from audience*): Ha, ha, ha!

(*Boy and Girl come dashing up to stage.*)

Boy and Girl (*together*):

We're not afraid of pumpkin heads,

For we are very wise.

We know that Jack-o'-lanterns can

Be turned to pumpkin pies.

Pumpkin Head (*aghast*):

What? You're not afraid of me?

Oh, dear, oh, dear! How can this be?

160

If I can't scare the likes of you
There's only one thing left to do:
Give up my spookiness and try
To turn myself to pumpkin pie.
(*He goes out, wailing.*)

Scarecrow (*coming forward waving his arms and speaking to audience*):
Of all the sillies I have met,
That pumpkin head's the silliest yet.
It's I who am the scariest one
As everybody knows,
A scarecrow's business is to scare
The everlasting crows.

Boy (*giving him a playful poke*):
We're not afraid of you at all!
You're only made of straw;
And clothes can never make a man.
That is a well-known law.

Scarecrow (*backing away a little*):
You're not afraid of staring eyes?
Or of my wicked grin?

Boy (*scornfully*):
They only need a pin.
That outfit doesn't scare the crows.
Why should it bother me?

Scarecrow (*weeping as he speaks*):
You're not afraid at all, I see . . .
I'm miserable as I can be.

Girl (*comfortingly*):
There, there, don't sob and cry!
There isn't any reason why

161

You *must* scare people with your staring.
You're very nice, though not too daring.
(*She pats him on the back.*)
Scarecrow (*still sobbing*):
Anyway, I'm through with scaring.
(*He goes out.*)
Witch (*coming forward and facing audience*):
The scarecrow and the pumpkin head
Have lived too long in error.
They thought they were ferocious folk,
But *I'm* the only terror!
I am a witch, a frightful witch.
I live up in a tree,
And everyone beneath the sun
Quakes at the sight of me.
(*She struts up and down the stage waving her broomstick, chanting.*)
I am a witch, a fearful witch.
I like to leap and fly
Upon a broom, where there is room
Up in the open sky.
(*She leaps and circles about.*)
The moon-man hides, the small stars shake
When I go dashing by,
For there is not in all the world
So wild a witch as I.
(*She stops, facing audience and teetering on her toes.*)
I am a witch, a frightful witch.
I live up in a tree,
And everyone beneath the sun
Quakes at the sight of me.
Boy (*indicating audience*):

162

Ha, ha! Ho, ho! Of all assembled
Not one has trembled.
(*He and Girl touch the witch.*)
Girl:
Hello, old witch, we do not fear you.
See! We dare to come quite near you!
Witch (*drawing back and waving her broom*):
Hocus, pocus, keep your distance!
This I say with great insistence.
Boy:
Are you trying just to joke us?
Girl:
There's no sense to "hocus pocus."
Witch (*retreating with a few backward steps*):
Don't you fear my hat and cape?
Or my ugliness and shape?
(*She points to caldron.*)
Aren't you just a bit afraid
Of the brew that I have made?
Aren't you frightened of my magic?
(*She is still moving backward and the children are getting closer to her.*)
This is getting very tragic.
(*She begins to sniffle.*)
What on earth can witches do
When the children . . .
Girl (*pouncing upon Witch*):
Just say, "BOO!"
(*Girl and Boy dance before the witch, laughing gaily.*)
Boy:
This will show how much we fear you.
Let the others all come near you.

163

(*Boy and Girl beckon offstage to Pumpkin Head and Scarecrow, who come back on stage and dance around Witch.*)
Spooks and witches may be cunning

Girl:
With their tricks and charms,

Pumpkin Head:
But Hallowe'en is made for funning—

Scarecrow:
Not for false alarms.

Witch (*suddenly nodding in approval, smiling and clapping her hands*):
Hallowe'en is made for prancing.
Let me join you in your dancing!
(*Witch joins Pumpkin Head and Scarecrow. They repeat the last two lines. Then all dance around merrily, as the curtain closes.*)

Scarecrow Puppet

Materials:
red print bandanna kerchief for shirt, or any colored fabric
blue print bandanna kerchief for trousers, or any colored fabric
burlap, or any fabric
colored construction paper, for hat
pencil
tracing paper
ruler
straight pins
scissors
needle and thread
Elmer's Glue-All

Directions:

HEAD:

1. Draw and cut out a 6 inch diameter paper circle (see Basic Shapes). Pin paper pattern on doubled piece of burlap. Cut around the pattern to make two circles. Remove the pins.

2. Turn down the edge of each circle and sew it down with running stitches. This will prevent unraveling. If you cannot sew, ask for help, or glue the edge down. Be sure both circles are the same size when they are finished.

3. Place both circles together with the sewed edges facing each other. Pin to hold. Sew around cloth with an overhand stitch. Leave an opening as large as your index finger. This will be the neck opening. When finished, the sewn burlap should be about $3\frac{1}{2}$ inches in diameter.

4. Stuff the burlap through the opening, with dried straw, dried leaves, dried corn husks, or torn strips of newspaper.

5. Trace Figure 1 to make a pattern for the hat (see Tracing Directions). Lay the pattern on a piece of colored construction paper, and hold it in place with a small piece of tape. Cut around the pattern. Remove tape. Try the pattern on the puppet's head for size. Remove and staple or glue the two edges together. Apply a dab of glue to the inner front and the back of the hat and place it on the puppet's head. Press the hat down snugly to hold. Cut the visor from a piece of construction paper of the same color. Glue it over the lower portion of the hat. Press to hold and allow it to dry.

6. Cut out two pieces of diamond-shaped scrap fabric to make the puppet's eyes. Glue them just below the visor.

7. A triangular piece of scrap fabric can be used for a nose. Glue it in place. Press to hold and allow to dry.

8. Crescent-shaped fabric can serve as a mouth, but you may

165

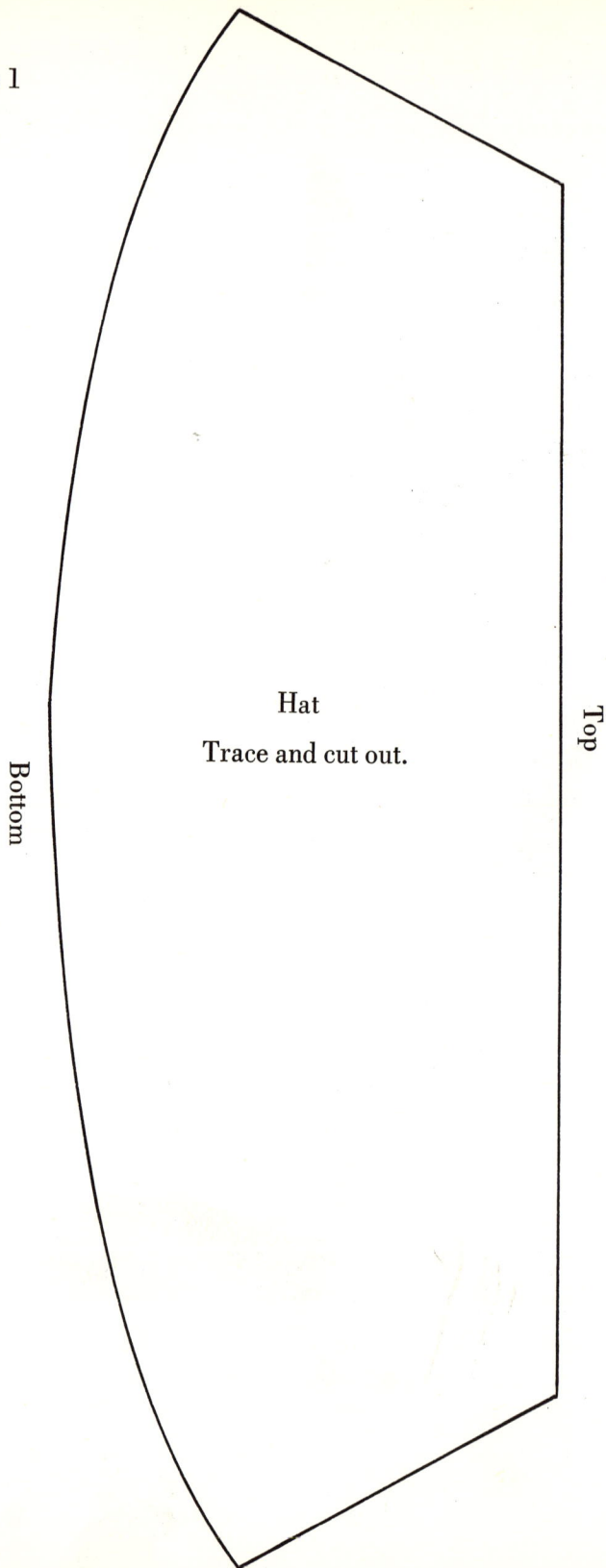

Figure 1

Hat

Trace and cut out.

Bottom

Top

prefer another shape. Glue the mouth on. Press to hold and allow to dry.

9. To make the puppet's neck, open an empty toilet-paper tube. Reroll it around your index finger for size. Measure it to make a tube about 4 inches long. Cut off excess cardboard. Glue and reroll to hold. Allow to dry. Apply glue around the upper neck tube, insert it into the neck opening at the base of head, turning it so that it fits snugly into the head. Allow a small portion to protrude from the bottom.

COSTUME:

1. Trace Figure 2 and make a full-sized pattern from it (see Tracing Directions).

2. Double the fabric with the wrong side out.

3. Lay the full-sized pattern on the doubled fabric and pin it down.

4. Cut the fabric around the pattern.

5. Remove pins and pattern.

6. Turn down the neck opening $\frac{1}{4}$ inch on each half of the wrong side, and sew with running stitches.

7. With the wrong side out, pin the two pieces of fabric together along shoulders, sleeves, and down the sides.

8. Baste $\frac{1}{4}$ inch from the edge along the shoulders, sleeves, and down the sides.

9. Remove pins.

10. Sew the sides together, following the basting, with running stitches.

11. Remove basting stitches.

12. Turn the shirt right-side out. Press if possible.

13. Trace Figure 3 and make a full-sized pattern for the trousers from it.

14. Transfer the pattern to fabric as you did in Steps 2 to 5.

167

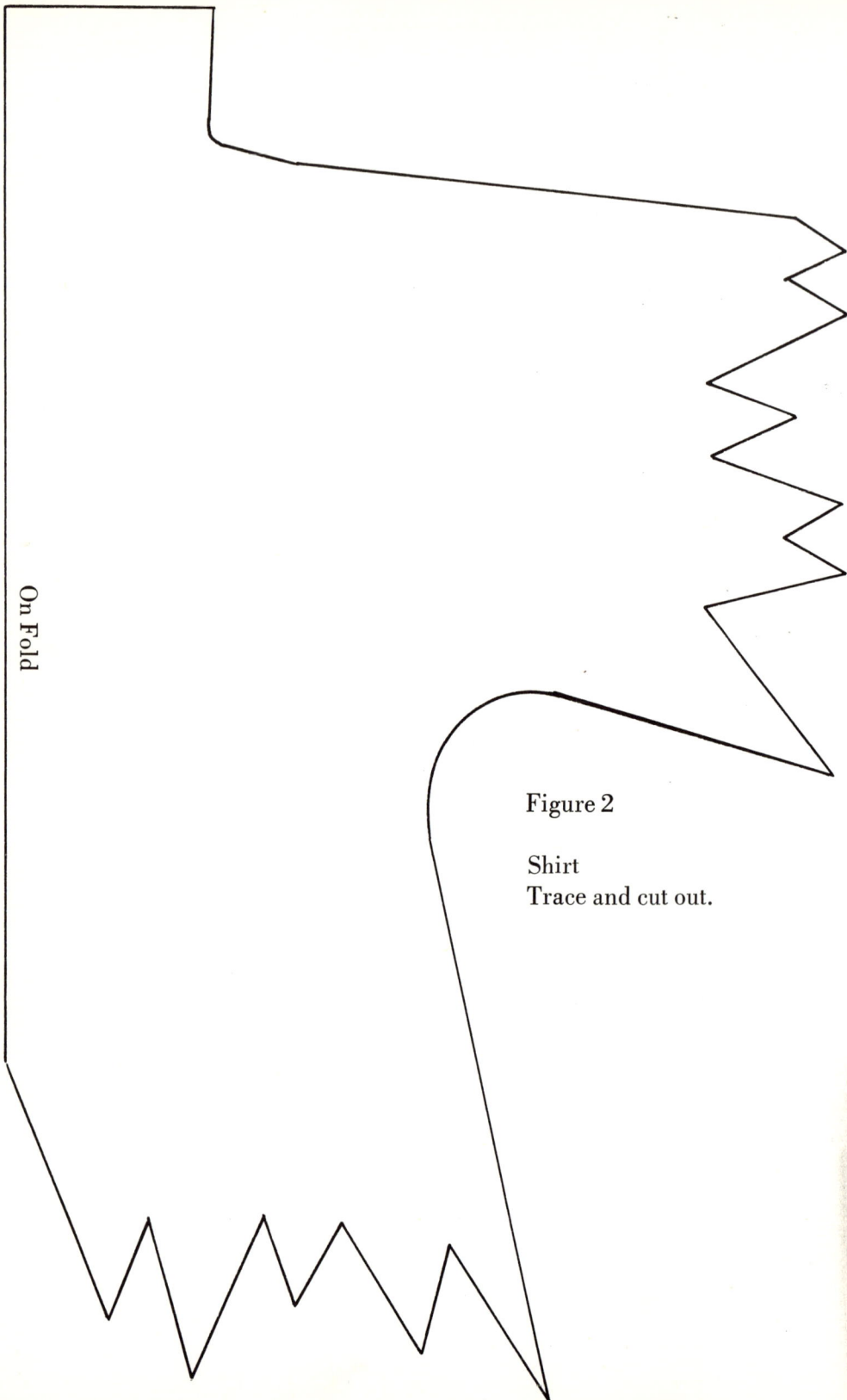

On Fold

Figure 2

Shirt
Trace and cut out.

Figure 3

Trousers
Trace and cut out.

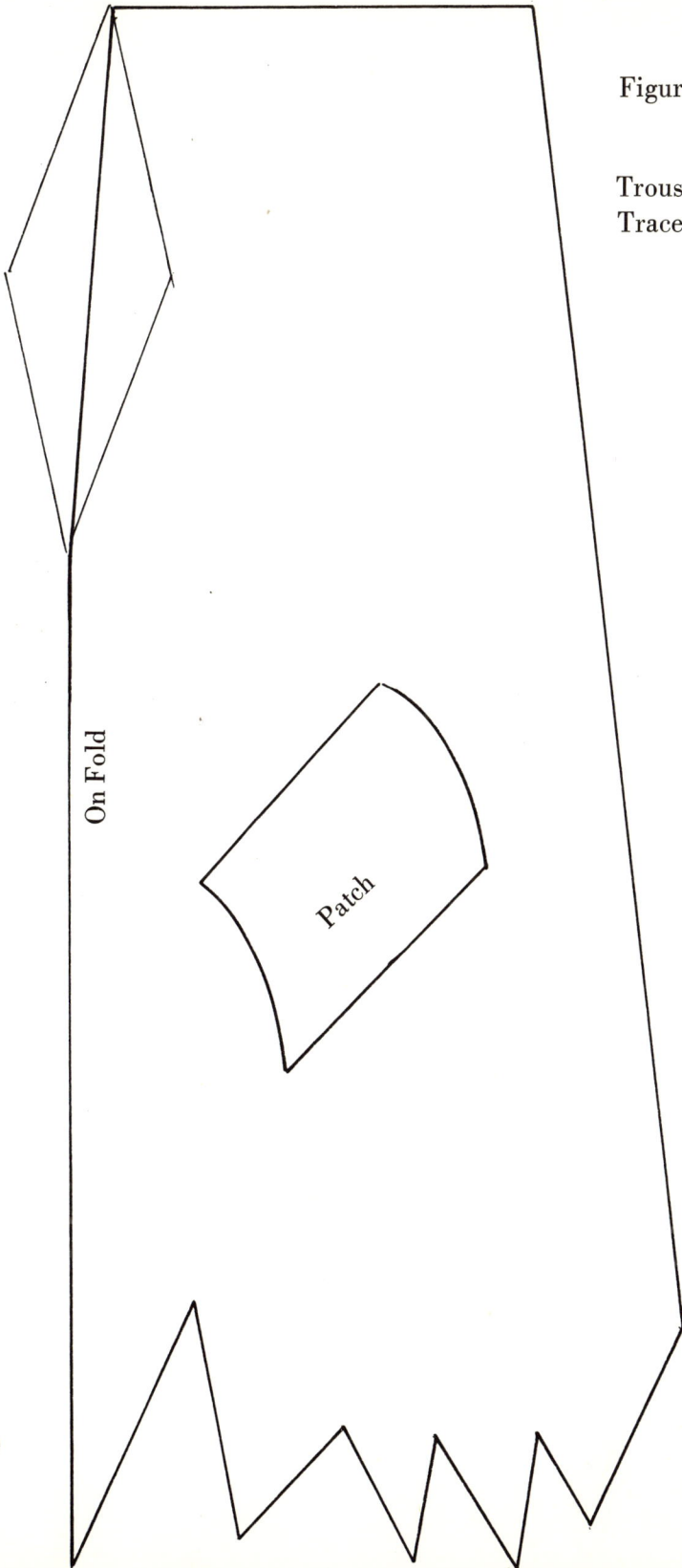

On Fold

Patch

15. Pin front and back together across the top and along the outer and inner edges of the legs.

16. Baste ¼ inch from edges.

17. Remove pins.

18. With running stitches, sew the top and outer and inner sides of each leg together.

19. Remove basting stitches.

20. Turn trousers right-side out. Press, if possible.

21. Slip the shirt over the trousers.

22. Pin the trousers to *front* of shirt only, at the waistline.

23. Sew the trousers to the shirt front with running stitches.

24. The trousers are closed at the top and attached to the front of shirt. This permits you to slip your hand under the shirt from the back to move the puppet.

25. Apply glue around the edge of the puppet's neck. Insert it into the shirt's neck opening. Press to hold. Allow to dry.

STUFFING THE PUPPET:

1. Stuff the puppet's trousers through the opening at the bottom of each leg. Use either dried straw, dried leaves, dried corn husks, or torn strips of newspaper. Allow some of the stuffing to show out of the bottom of each leg opening.

2. Stuff each sleeve through the opening with the same stuffing. Stuffing should go from one sleeve, across front, to other sleeve. Allow some to show out of each sleeve opening.

DECORATING:

Fill the opening at the top of hat with dried straw, dried corn husks, dried leaves, dried wild flowers, dried rose hips, dried bittersweet, or strips of newspaper. Some of the ends can be pushed through the crown, over the eyes for hair. The other ends stick up straight out of the top opening of hat. For a beard, apply glue to small pieces of pine needles and insert through front neck opening of the burlap face. Press

170

to hold. Allow to dry. You may use other materials for beard, such as fringed black crepe or construction paper, or pieces of black yarn.

Holding the Scarecrow Puppet for Action:
1. Place your hand inside the puppet through the opening at the bottom of the shirt.
2. Place your index finger up through the neck tube and inside the head.
3. Insert your thumb in one sleeve and your middle finger in the other.
4. Your thumb and middle finger become the puppet's arms.
5. Move your thumb and middle finger to make the puppet's arms move. Move your index finger to make the puppet's head move from side to side or up and down.

Witch Puppet

In pioneer days a mother often carved out an apple face to entertain her children. If left on a windowsill for a few weeks the apple head would look like a shriveled-up old woman. This led to an early American hobby of making apple-head figures.

Materials:
apple—Baldwin or Winesap are best
lemon juice
knives—small paring knife for peeling, curved grapefruit
    knife, if available, for carving
dowel on stand
brown fabric
black fabric
black construction paper
black poster board

171

black knitting yarn or crepe paper for hair

tracing paper

pencil

scissors

straight pins

Elmer's Glue-All

needle and black thread if costume is to be sewn

stapler and staples if costume is to be stapled

Directions:

HEAD:

1. Peel the apple.

2. Taper the lower third of the apple to make a chin if you wish, but this is not necessary.

3. At the bottom of the apple, carve out a neck hole large enough so that you can insert your index finger into it.

4. Outline features in pencil, using Figures 1 to 5 as guides.

5. Press two small pupils, consisting of colored pieces of glass, wood, pebbles, or large pinheads, where each eye socket will be carved.

6. Carve out the eyes (Figure 1) around the pupils. Do not insert the knife too deeply.

7. Carve out the nose (Figure 2).

8. Carve out the mouth (Figure 3).

9. Carve out the cheekbones (Figure 4). After you've carved all the features, the apple should look like Figure 5.

10. When carving is completed, dip the apple in lemon juice.

11. Place the apple-head upright on a dowel with a stand, and allow it to dry.

12. Keep it in a dry, airy place or on a radiator for about four weeks. It will be fascinating to see how the features change as the apple shrinks. Since no two apples shrivel up exactly alike, it is advisable to carve and dry two or three

172

Figure 1  Cut away.

Figure 2 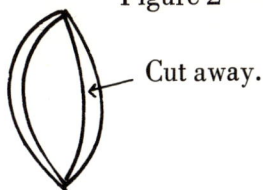 Cut away.

Figure 3 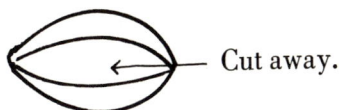 Cut away.

Figure 4 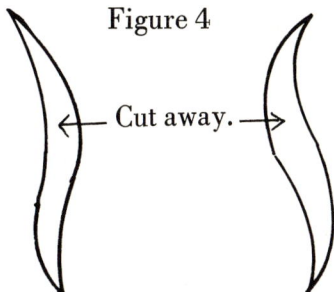 Cut away.

Carve out eyes, nose, mouth, and cheekbones.

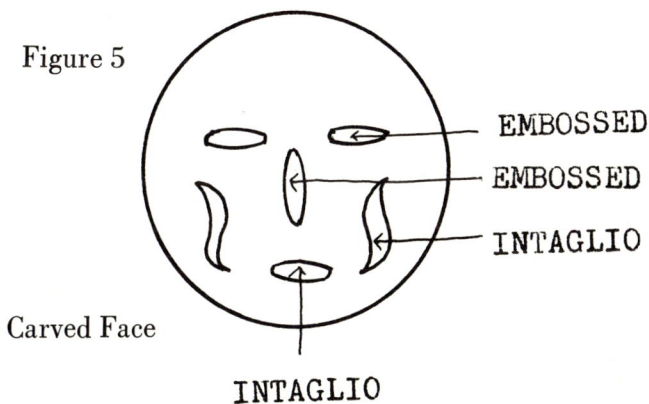

Figure 5

EMBOSSED
EMBOSSED
INTAGLIO

Carved Face

INTAGLIO

apples, and then select the most interesting one for the witch.
13. After the apple dries, open an empty toilet-paper tube.
Roll it tightly around your index finger and cut it down to
4 inches. Glue the edges and roll it up again. After it dries,
insert it into the neck opening of the apple, allowing a small
portion to protrude from the bottom.

173

HAIR:

1. Keep the apple head on the stand while applying 5-inch strands of black yarn for hair.

2. Apply glue to the top, sides, and back of the head. Starting at the side, attach one strand of black yarn at a time around the head.

3. When it is dry, trim if necessary.

HAT:

1. Draw and cut out a circle about 3 inches in diameter from black poster board (see Basic Shapes).

2. Using black construction paper, make a cone from half of a $5\frac{1}{2}$ inch circle to make the crown.

3. Apply glue around the cone opening and position it in the center of the 3 inch disk. Press to hold. Allow to dry.

4. Apply glue to the center of the brim. Position the hat on the witch's head. Press to hold. Allow to dry.

COSTUME:

1. Trace Figure 6 and make a full pattern from it (see Tracing Directions). Transfer the pattern to two pieces of brown fabric.

2. Turn down the neck opening, sleeves, and hem of each half, $\frac{1}{4}$ inch, on the wrong side and sew the edges down with running stitches.

3. Sew the two sides of the costume together, using running stitches.

4. Apply glue around the outer wall of the puppet's neck. Insert it into the neck of the dress. Press the dress opening around the neck tube. Allow to dry.

5. Make a pattern for the cape from a paper semicircle with a $6\frac{1}{2}$ inch radius.

6. Lay the pattern on black fabric. Pin it down. Cut it out. Remove the pins and the pattern.

174

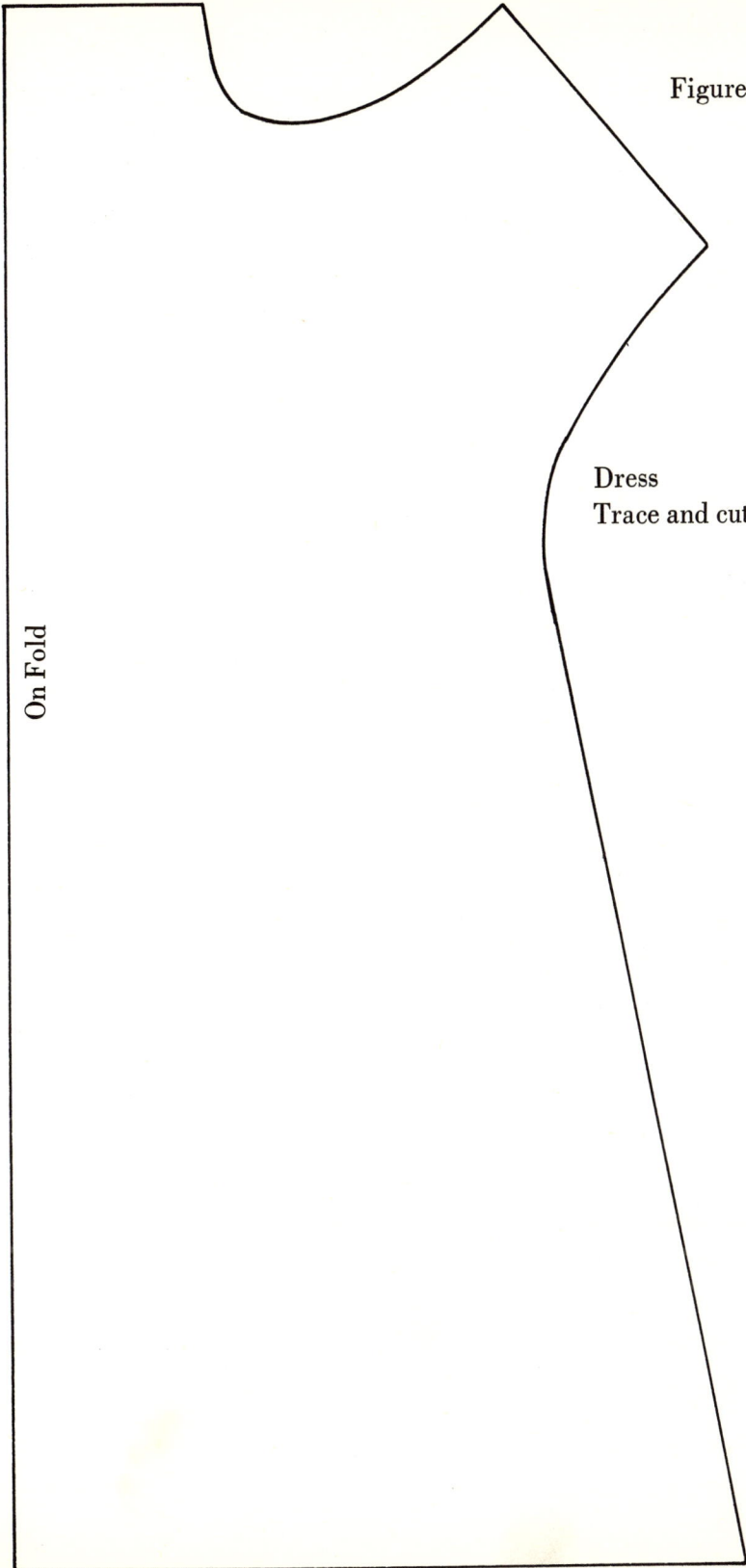

Figure 6

Dress
Trace and cut out.

On Fold

7. Turn down the edge of the straight side of the semicircle and sew it with running stitches. Do not cut the thread.
8. Pull the thread evenly on both sides and gather the cape around the witch. Tie the ends of the thread securely around the neck. Trim off excess thread.

Holding the Witch Puppet for Action:
Follow Steps 1 to 4 for the Scarecrow to hold and move the Witch hand puppet.

Pumpkin Puppet

Materials:
construction paper, orange
construction paper, yellow
cardboard or poster board, any color
crepe paper, green, brown
Elmer's Glue-All
scissors
ruler
pencil
tracing paper

Directions:
HEAD:
1. Trace Figure 1 and transfer the tracing to another sheet to make a full-sized pattern (see Tracing Directions). Cut out five sections from orange construction paper.
2. Lay each section on the table with the points overlapping, like petals.
3. Apply glue on the tip of one section and under the tips of each succeeding overlapping section. Press to hold and allow to dry.

176

Figure 1

On Fold

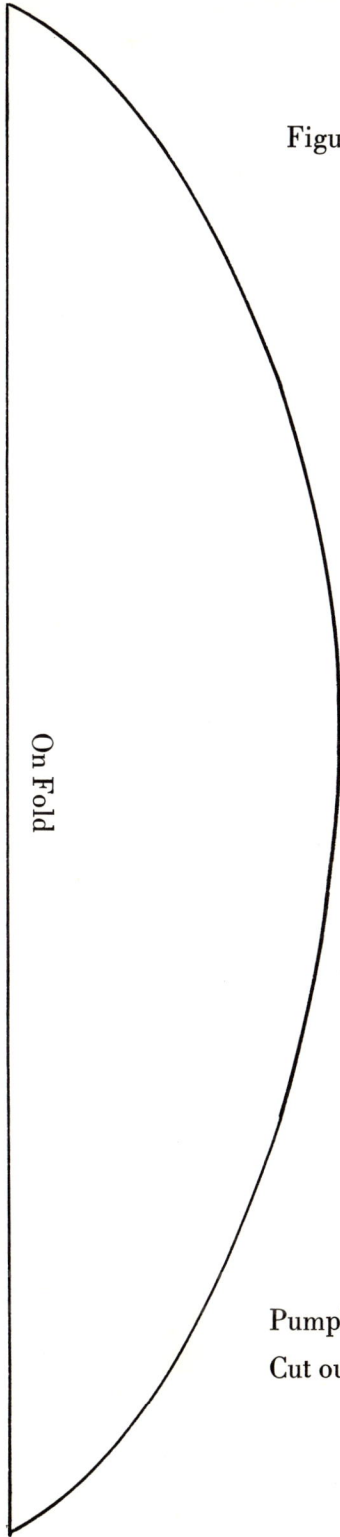

Pumpkin-Head Section
Cut out five.

4. For the neck, make a cylinder from a strip of cardboard or poster board, $1\frac{1}{2}$ inches wide and long enough to go around your hand when it is finished (see Basic Shapes).

5. Attach the petal-shaped figure to the neck cylinder. To do so, apply glue under the free tip of each orange segment. Glue the segments, evenly spaced, over the lower edge of the neck cylinder. Press each section and allow it to dry. Now you have a pumpkinlike shape.

6. For hair, cut strips of brown crepe paper or construction paper, about $\frac{3}{4}$ inch wide and 5 or 4 inches long. Curl the paper over a pencil or scissor blade (see Paper Techniques). Apply glue to one end of each strip and drape the strips around the head, but do not glue hair strips over one segment. This will be the face.

7. To make a hat brim, draw a 5 inch diameter circle on yellow cardboard or poster board.

8. Using construction paper of the same color, make a cylinder from a 10 by 2 inch strip, gluing the 2 inch edges together. Slash several $\frac{1}{2}$ inch tabs at one edge of the cylinder. Fold each tab. Glue the tabs to the brim (see Figure 2). Press to hold and allow to dry.

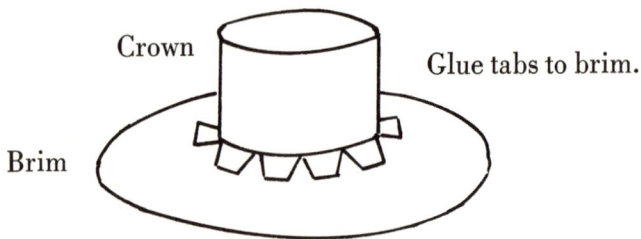

Crown

Glue tabs to brim.

Brim

Pumpkin's Hat, Assembled

9. To attach the hat to the head, apply glue to the center of the brim. Place the hat at an angle over the pumpkin's hair.

Hold it in place until it dries.

10. Make a nose from a 2 by 2 by 2 inch triangle of yellow construction paper. Glue it on, and hold it in place until it dries.

11. Draw and cut out a mouth, using yellow construction paper. Glue it on. Press to hold. Allow to dry. The corners of the mouth should extend slightly beyond the edges of one segment.

12. Two diamond- or triangle-shaped pieces of yellow construction paper can be the pumpkin's eyes. Cut out two smaller pieces of black construction paper for pupils. Glue each pupil on one yellow diamond or triangle. Glue one eye piece on each side of the nose. The corners of each eye piece will fall slightly beyond the front pumpkin segment.

13. Make a necktie from a strip of green crepe paper, $2\frac{1}{2}$ by 10 inches. Fold it in half to make a $1\frac{1}{4}$ inch strip. Apply glue to one side. Wind it around the neck cylinder. Cut another strip of green crepe paper and make a bow. Tie a piece of thread around the middle. Apply glue to one side. Position it on the neck cylinder under the mouth. Hold it in place until it dries. This completes the pumpkin puppet, as it does not need to be dressed.

Holding the Pumpkin Puppet for Action:

1. To use the pumpkin as a hand puppet, insert your hand through the neck opening at the bottom. Turn your hand from side to side or up and down for movement.

2. To use it as a rod puppet, attach it to a narrow rod about 11 inches long. Apply glue to one end of rod. Position this end to front, inner side of neck cylinder. Press to hold. Allow to dry. Hold the other end of the rod in your fingers, and twirl it from side to side.

179

Production Notes

Scenery and Properties:

The play takes place in a field with trees fastened to the floor and painted on a backdrop. The witch's caldron is made from black poster board. Her broomstick is a small narrow dowel, painted black. A fringe of black crepe paper is glued to one end of the broomstick. You can also attach pieces of broom straw to the broomstick.

Action:

A boy and girl from the audience stand in front of the puppet stage and perform with the puppets. The witch stirs the caldron with her broom until she comes forward to say her piece.

THANKSGIVING DAY

Unexpected Guests

A I L E E N   F I S H E R

Characters:
Governor Bradford
Miles Standish
Mistress Brewster
Mistress Winslow
Priscilla
Desire
William
Other Boy

Properties:
list on wall
table with small plates and food stuff
open door
bucket
wood

Prologue

Setting:
In front of the curtain. Governor Bradford and Miles Standish walk in, talking to each other. They cross slowly in front of the curtain.

Gov. Bradford: We have had our trials in this new land, Captain Standish. Our hardships. Our sorrows. But how much we have to be thankful for!

Miles Standish: Aye, Governor Bradford.

Gov. Bradford: Nowhere in England could we have grown such a crop of corn on twenty acres.

Miles Standish: That is true. And such barley! (*Sniffs the air*). I smell barley loaves baking this very minute. Ah, and pigeon pasty, too, I do believe.

Gov. Bradford: 'Tis a busy day today in Plymouth town. Think you Chief Massasoit and some of his braves will heed our invitation to join in the feast of thanksgiving?

Miles Standish: Aye, a few will come, I believe, Governor. The Indians have been very friendly.

Gov. Bradford: Another thing to be thankful for. Our cup is indeed full. (As they exit) Shall we see if the tables are properly set up under the trees, and the meat-spits ready?

Act I

At Curtain Rise:

We see a kitchen-living room of one of the Pilgrim houses. Mistress Brewster is working at the table where food for the feast is being prepared. In a moment Mistress Winslow hurries in.

Mistress Winslow: Good day, Mistress Brewster.

Mistress Brewster: Good morning to you.
And, oh, Mistress Winslow,
There's *still* much to do.
As sure as I'm living
This feast of Thanksgiving
Takes planning and hustling
And labor . . .

Mistress Winslow: How true! (*She consults list on wall.*)
Let's see what is finished.
The pies are all made,
Both pumpkin and berry.
The tables are laid? (*Glances out window to see*)
The loaves are a-baking
Next door, no mistaking. (*Sniffs, turns back to list*)
The turkeys need stuffing,
And soon, I'm afraid.
(*Priscilla and Desire hurry in to help.*)

Girls: Good morning, good morning.
Thanksgiving is here!

Mistress Brewster: The busiest morning,
For us, of the year.
Desire, grind corn and don't tarry.
Priscilla, shell beechnuts
For stuffing, my dear.
(*Desire and Priscilla go to the table and busy themselves.*)

Priscilla: The boys were to help us.
They're always so slow! (*Looks around*)
The woodpile has vanished.
The water is low.
That William—where is he?
(*William and another boy hurry in.*)

Boys (*Cheerfully*): Good morning.

Priscilla: Get busy,
There's company coming
For dinner, you know.
(*Mistress Brewster gives empty bucket to one boy to get water. She then puts William to work helping Priscilla husk beechnuts.*)

Mistress Brewster: Desire, start taking
The platters outside—

183

The fruits we have gathered
And carefully dried,
The grapes and the cherries,
The nuts and the berries . . . (Desire goes in and out.)

William (*hungrily*): I'm thankful the platters
Are big ones and wide!

Mistress Winslow: We all can be thankful
This bright autumn morn—

Priscilla: For Squanto—who taught us
The way to plant corn.
For rain and for weather and crops
And being together!

Mistress Brewster: For finding a homeland
Where faith is reborn.
(*They all work busily. Suddenly William, looking over the
food supply, gets worried.*)

William: I say, Mistress Brewster,
Would we be prepared.
To feed twenty Indians?

Mistress Brewster: Our feast may be shared
With ten or with twenty,
And there will be plenty.

William: But what if there's *thirty?*

Mistress Brewster: I think we'll be spared.
Miles Standish thinks maybe
A dozen might come.

Mistress Winslow: We Pilgrims are fifty.
That makes quite a lot. (*Looks over food*)
But surely there's ample
For more than a sample
Of dozens of good things . . . (*Turns to William*)
Just look in the pot.

(*Boy comes back with water, then with wood. Mistress Brewster then puts him in charge of fire.*)

Boy: It keeps us all hopping,
This having a feast. (*Miles Standish hurries in, looks around anxiously.*)

Miles Standish: These lads—are they needed?
One boy must be speeded
To gather more clams
From the cove to the east.
(Boys are eager to go.)

Mistress Brewster: Two lads, Captain Standish?
Well, if it seems fit . . .

Miles Standish: The other should handle
The meat-turning spit
And keep the fires going
So coals will be glowing
For roasting the oysters.

Mistress Brewster: Grave tasks, I admit. (*Mistress Brewster nods to boys, dismissing them. They hurry out with Miles Standish. Mistress Winslow checks the list again.*)

Mistress Winslow: The wild geese and turkeys
Are ready to stuff.
The stuffing, Priscilla?

Priscilla: Will this be enough?

Mistress Winslow: Perhaps, but I doubt it.

Priscilla: Well, I'll go without it.

Mistress Brewster (nervously): I'm hoping these dumplings won't sink and be tough. (*All work busily. In a few minutes the sound of shouting is heard offstage. The women and girls are startled.*)

Girls: What's that? Someone's shouting.

Women: How lusty and loud!

Girls: It may be the Indians.

It sounds like a crowd.

(*William rushes in excitedly.*)

William: Our guests are arriving! (*He keeps looking out the door, turning back to report as more and more Indians arrive.*)

The Indians! I'm striving

To count. At least thirty

Brave warriors and proud . . .

Now forty . . . now fifty . . .

Now *sixty* . . .

Mistress Brewster (*Unbelieving*): Don't joke!

William: Now seventy crowding

There under the oak.

And still they keep coming!

Mistress Brewster: My poor ears are humming.

Mistress Winslow: How can we, how *can* we

Feed so many folk?

William: Eighty. No, *ninety!*

Chief Massasoit too.

Mistress Brewster: We figured a dozen . . .

Oh, what shall we do?

Mistress Winslow: For all our preparing,

The food we'll be sharing

Will scarcely be ample

To last the day through.

Desire: And they were invited

To stay for *three days.*

Mistress Brewster: My head's in a turmoil.

Mistress Winslow: My mind's in a haze.

Girls: We're all in a dither—

From whence and from whither

Shall we get more turkeys,
More meat, and more maize?

William (*Excitedly, from post at door*): There's Governor
Bradford. He's coming.

Mistress Brewster: Poor man,
He's probably worried.
Let's smile . . . if we can.

Gov. Bradford (*Hurrying in*):
Dear ladies, I wonder,
Would it be a blunder
To ask you a favor,
A slight change of plan?
The Indians are eager
To help and to share:
They want to bring deer-meat
To add to our fare.
But after your labors
To feed our good neighbors
I felt I should ask you,
Dear friends, if you'd *care?*
They'll handle the roasting.
It might be a treat . . .
Unless you prefer
Our own foodstuffs to eat.

Girls (*gaily*): With deer-meat aplenty
We'll feed eight times twenty!

Women (*graciously*): Indeed, it will make our
Thanksgiving complete.
(*Governor Bradford nods, and goes out.*)

Girls (*amused*): He asked if we minded!
These innocent men . . .

Women (*amused*): You'd think we had *counted*

187

On ninety, not ten.
All: But now, as we're living,
  We'll have a thanksgiving
  To speak of with pleasure
  Again and again . . .
  A feast-day we'll treasure
  Again and again!
  (*Curtain draws*)

Pilgrim Lady

Materials:
brown or gray crepe paper or fabric
white felt
discarded nylon stocking
paper towels, newspaper, or tissue paper
poster board, color of your choice
tracing paper
scissors
Elmer's Glue-All
pencil
ruler
needle and thread
small piece blue construction paper

Directions:
HEAD:
1. Make the puppet's neck from an empty tube of toilet paper. Open the tube and roll it around your index finger. Measure a 3 inch piece, remove it while it is still rolled, and cut off the excess. Glue it securely. Apply glue to the outer surface of half the tube.

188

2. Wrap paper towels or newspaper around the glued portion of the neck tube until you have a $2\frac{1}{2}$ inch diameter ball.

3. Tie the paper ball around the upper part of the neck securely. Dab it with glue if necessary.

4. Stuff the paper ball and neck tube into the toes of a nylon stocking.

5. Pull the stocking snugly over it and tie it around the neck, just under the ball of paper.

6. Cut off the remainder of the stocking a little below the end of tube.

7. Gather the loose nylon around the neck tube and dab it with glue to prevent it from running.

HAIR:

1. Trace Figure 1 (see Tracing Directions).

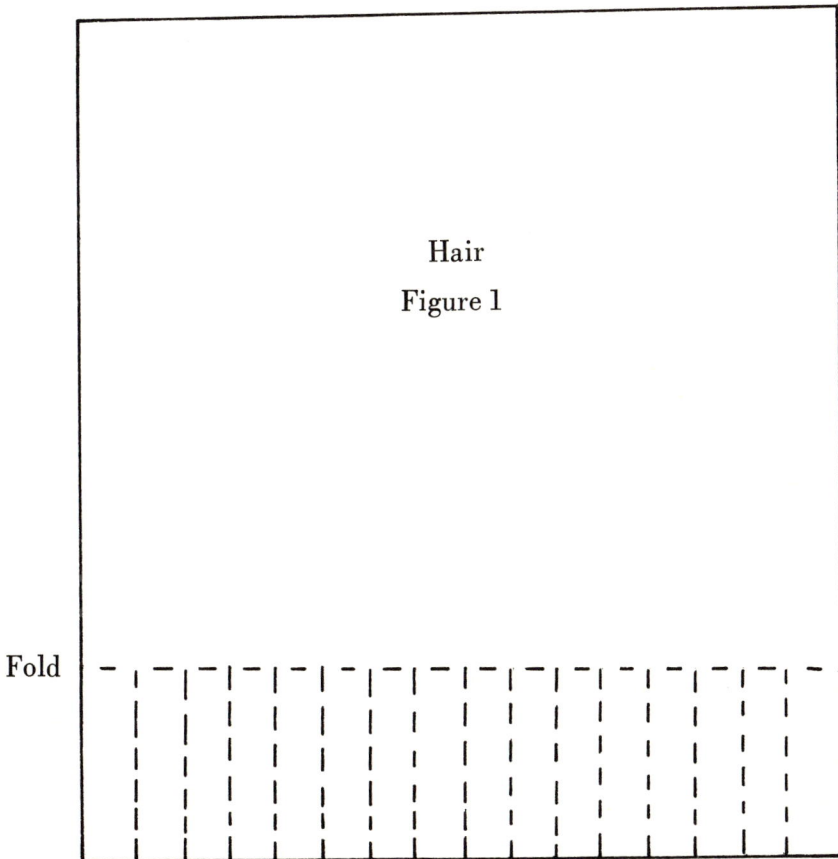

Hair

Figure 1

Fold

Trace and cut out.   Cut dotted lines for fringe.

2. Lay the pattern on the fold of brown crepe paper and pin it.

3. Cut around the pattern, but do not cut the fold. Cut dotted lines. Remove pins.

4. Open crepe paper and apply glue to the unfringed side.

5. Lay the piece over the head with the fringes draped over the forehead and sides. Gather and drape the unfringed side at the back. Allow it to dry.

FACIAL FEATURES:

1. Trace Figure 2 to make eyes. Transfer the pattern to black construction paper. Cut out two. Glue one to each side, holding them in place with straight pins until they are dry.

2. Draw eyebrows with a black flair pen.

3. Draw the nose with a black flair pen.

4. Draw a mouth with a red flair pen, or draw a mouth on red construction paper, cut it out, and glue it on the face.

HEADBAND:

1. Trace Figure 3 to make a pattern and transfer it to poster board.

2. Apply glue on back of one side and place it over the puppet's head, as shown in the photograph. Press and secure it by pushing straight pins into the top and sides through the wadded paper.

DRESS:

1. Cut a piece of crepe paper or fabric, 25 by 8½ inches.

2. Glue the two short edges together, allowing one edge to overlap the other.

3. Place the crepe paper on the table and cut out two arm holes, one on each side.

4. Turn down the edge around each armhole, about ¼ inch, and glue it to hold. This will prevent the paper from tearing with use.

190

Trace and cut out.

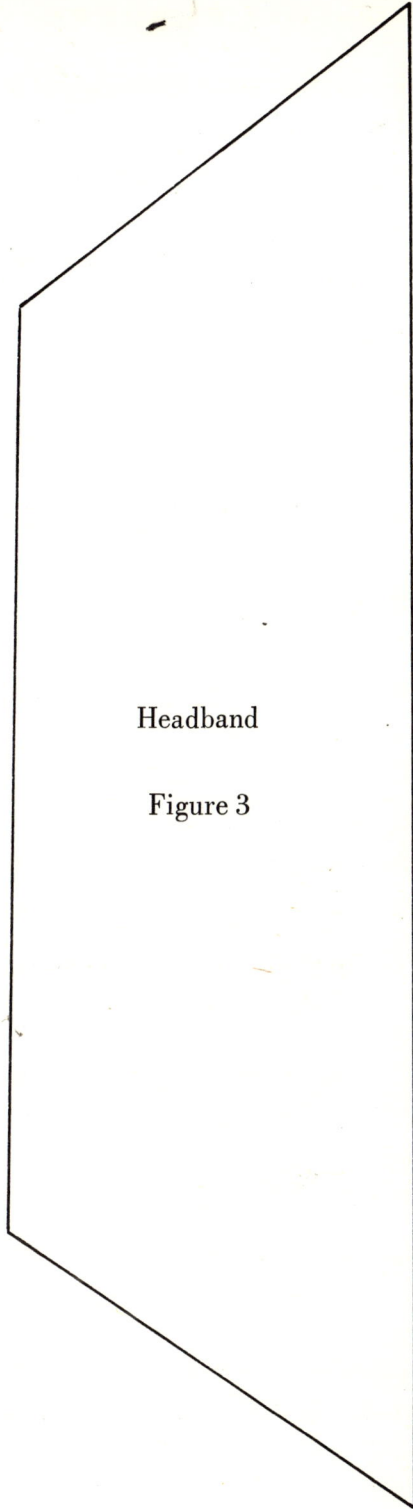

Eye

Figure 2

Back

Front

Trace and cut out.

Headband

Figure 3

5. Gather the crepe paper at the top opening with running stitches, $\frac{1}{2}$ inch from the edge.

6. Insert the puppet's neck into the gathered end and gently pull the thread around it so that the gathered paper fits snugly around the neck tube. Be sure the arm openings are on the sides.

7. Wind the thread that is still on the needle around the puppet's neck several times. Tack it to the nylon covering before cutting the thread from the needle.

SHAWL:

1. Trace Figure 4. Pin the pattern to a doubled piece of crepe paper. Cut it out. Remove pins and pattern. Open the crepe-paper shawl to full size.

2. Dab glue under the back and two front sides.

3. Drape it around the puppet's shoulders, overlapping the two front pieces. Press the back and front to the puppet's dress to hold. Allow it to dry.

4. To make the collar trace Figure 5 and transfer the pattern to a piece of white felt. Cut it out, making a slit in back, as shown. Drape the collar around the neck and glue it in place.

Holding the Puppet for Action:

The puppet is held and moved the same way as the Pilgrim Man (next puppet), except that your thumb and middle fingers go through the armholes of the dress.

Pilgrim Man

Materials:
brown felt
brown crepe paper or fabric
white felt or construction paper

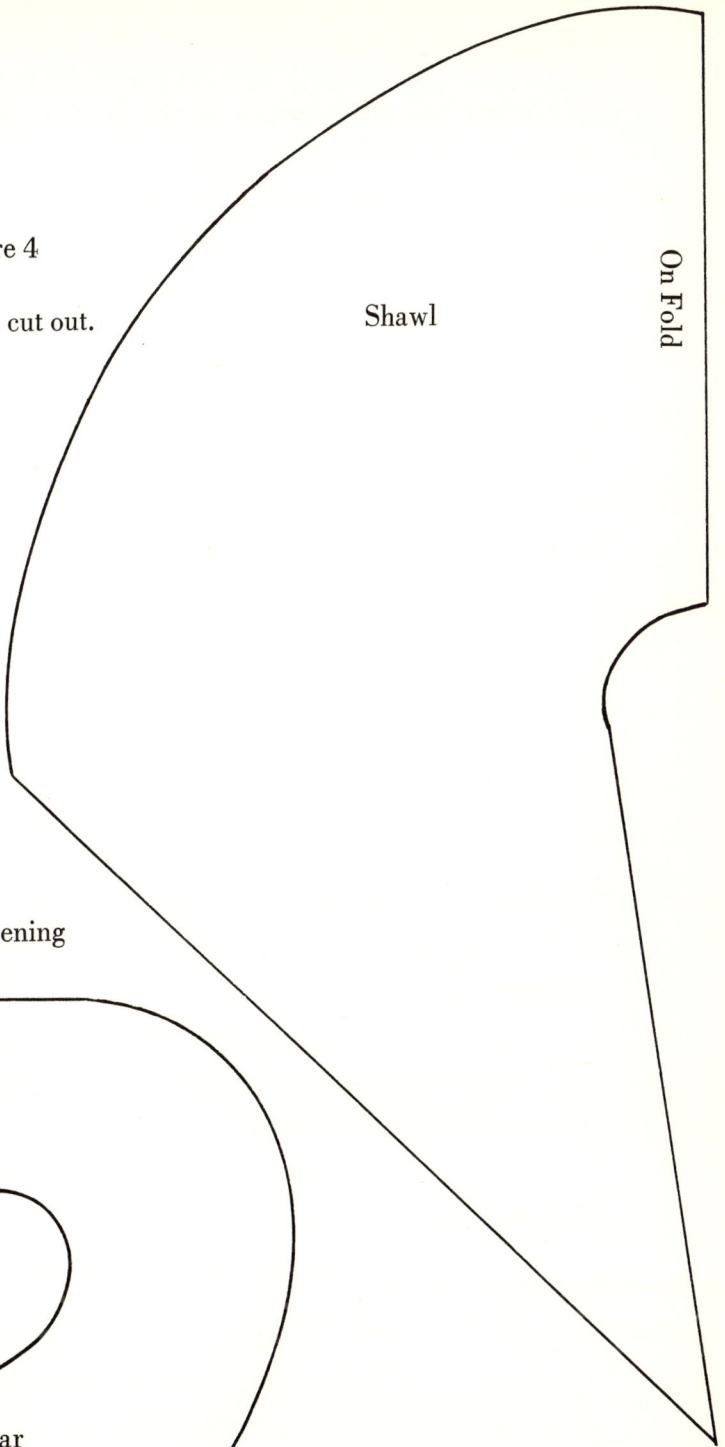

Figure 4

Trace and cut out.

Shawl

On Fold

Back opening

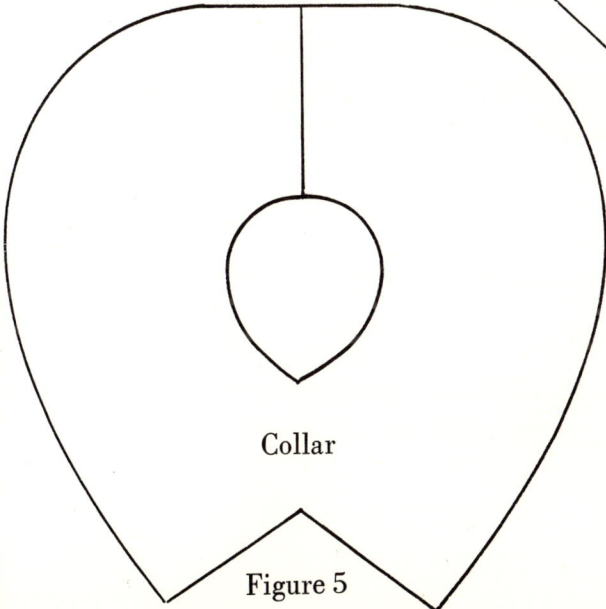

Collar

Figure 5

Trace and cut solid lines.

discarded nylon stocking
paper towels, newspaper, or tissue paper
black construction paper
tracing paper
scissors
Elmer's Glue-All
pencil
ruler
needle and black thread
stapler and staples
several straight pins

Directions:

BREECHES:

1. Cut a piece of crepe paper, 11 by $9\frac{1}{2}$ inches.

2. Roll the $9\frac{1}{2}$ inch end loosely.

3. Gather each end tightly together.

4. Cut two 1 by 9 inch strips of crepe paper.

5. Wind one strip around each end of the crepe-paper roll several times and glue to secure.

6. Fold the roll in half to form two legs.

CHEST:

1. Cut a piece of crepe paper, 10 by 12 inches. Fold the 10 inch side in half so that you have a doubled 5 inch width.

2. Apply glue to lower edge, and wrap the crepe around the folded upper $1\frac{1}{4}$ inch of the breeches. Wrap it around.

3. Dab glue to the open side. Press it to the rolled crepe paper to close.

4. Staple the top together.

5. Puff out each leg by stuffing pieces of crepe paper through openings at the sides. Glue each side opening down. Figure 1 shows the assembled Pilgrim-man frame.

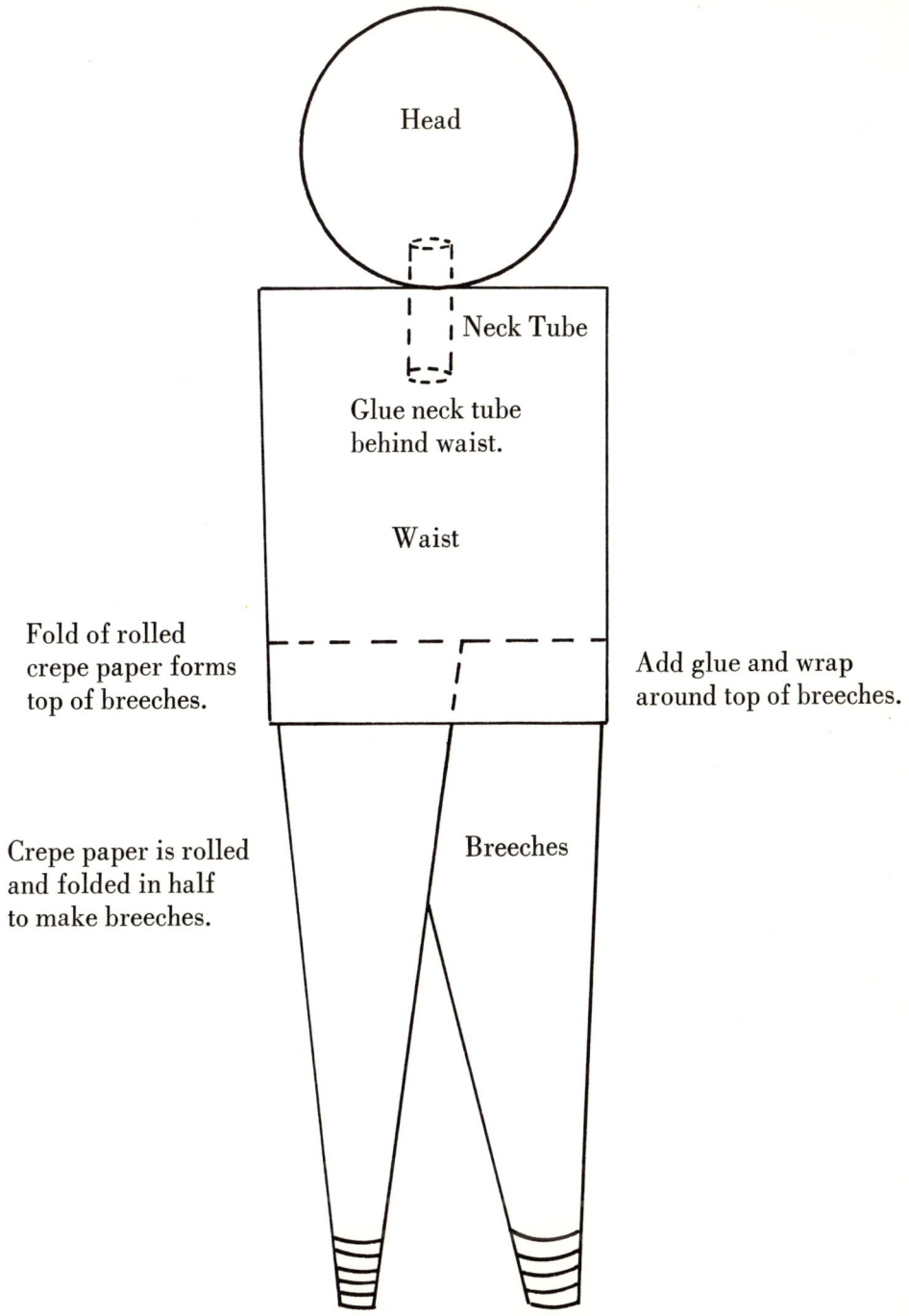

Head

Neck Tube

Glue neck tube
behind waist.

Waist

Fold of rolled
crepe paper forms
top of breeches.

Add glue and wrap
around top of breeches.

Crepe paper is rolled
and folded in half
to make breeches.

Breeches

Frame

Figure 1

TUNIC:

1. Trace Figure 2 and transfer the half pattern to another sheet to make a full-sized pattern.

2. Cut a piece of brown felt, 12 by 9 inches. Fold the 12 inch side in half. Lay the full-sized pattern with the shoulders on the fold.

3. Pin together. Cut out the pattern. Remove pins and pattern.

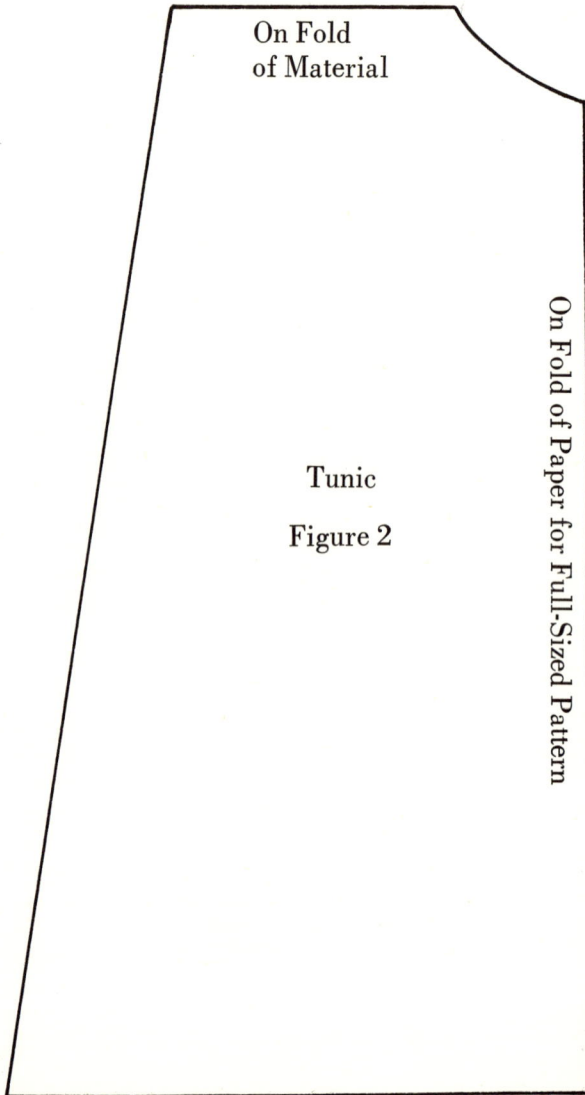

On Fold
of Material

On Fold of Paper for Full-Sized Pattern

Tunic

Figure 2

Trace and cut out.

4. Cut two narrow strips of felt about 2½ inches long. Pin one end of the strip halfway up at the side of tunic front; pin the other end of the strip to the back. Do the same with the other side.

5. Staple or sew each end to the tunic front and back. If you sew it, use overhand stitches. Remove pins.

6. Slip the tunic over the top of crepe-paper chest.

7. Staple front neck opening of tunic to top of chest, allowing the back of tunic to remain open so that you can slip your hand through.

HEAD:

1. Follow Steps 1 to 7 for the Pilgrim Lady.

2. To attach the head to the tunic, apply glue around the base of the neck tube. Insert it through the neck opening at the top of the tunic, *behind* the top of chest. This will attach the front of the neck to the chest.

3. Press the front and back of tunic to the necktube. Allow to dry.

HAIR:

1. Trace Figure 1 for Pilgrim Lady's hair and follow Steps 1 to 4. However, the Pilgrim man's hair is attached differently. The unfringed side is draped over the front of the head. The fringed side is draped at the sides and back of the head. Allow to dry.

HAT:

1. Trace Figures 3 and 4 to make patterns for brim and crown of the hat.

2. Lay the half-sized pattern of Figure 3 on the fold of a doubled piece of black construction paper. Use a piece of masking tape to hold. Trace and cut. Lay the full-sized pattern of Figure 4 on black construction paper. Hold, trace, and cut.

3. Fold bottom tabs.

On Fold   On Fold

Hat Brim

Figure 3

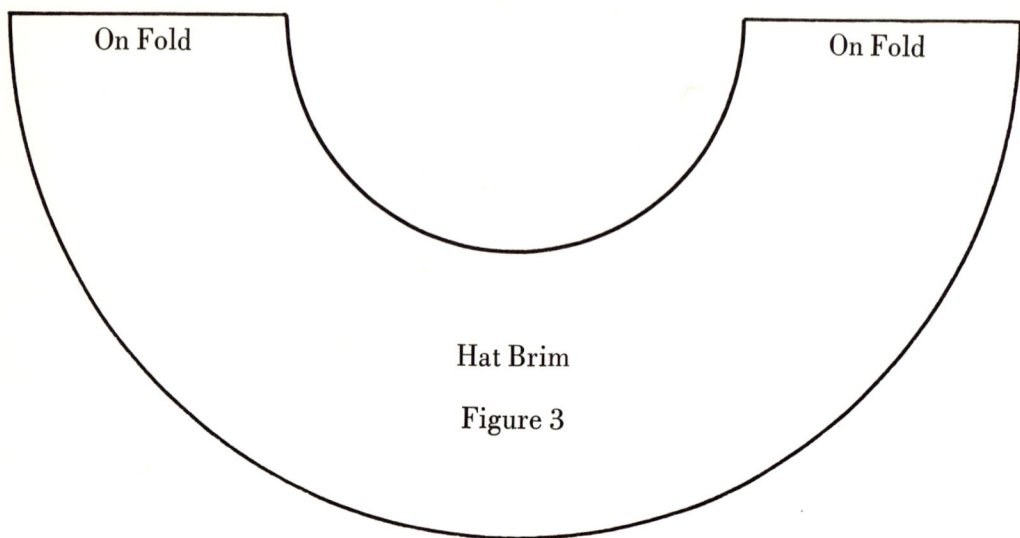

Trace and cut out.

4. Glue and close the edges of the crown.
5. Insert the top of crown into the brim opening, up to the tabs. Be sure it fits snugly.
6. Apply glue underneath each tab. Press tabs against the brim. Allow to dry.

These dimensions may not be exactly right for your puppet's head. If your puppet's head is larger, you will need a larger brim opening and crown tube. If smaller, the brim opening must be smaller and the crown must be a narrower tube. Be sure the opening of the brim fits snugly over the puppet's head.
7. Cut a 1 by ½ inch piece of white construction paper. Cut out a smaller piece of black construction paper of the same shape.
8. Glue the black piece in the center of white piece.

Overlapping tab

Tab

Cut away.

Tab

Cut away.

Form cylinder, apply glue to tabs,
insert in brim, and press to hold.

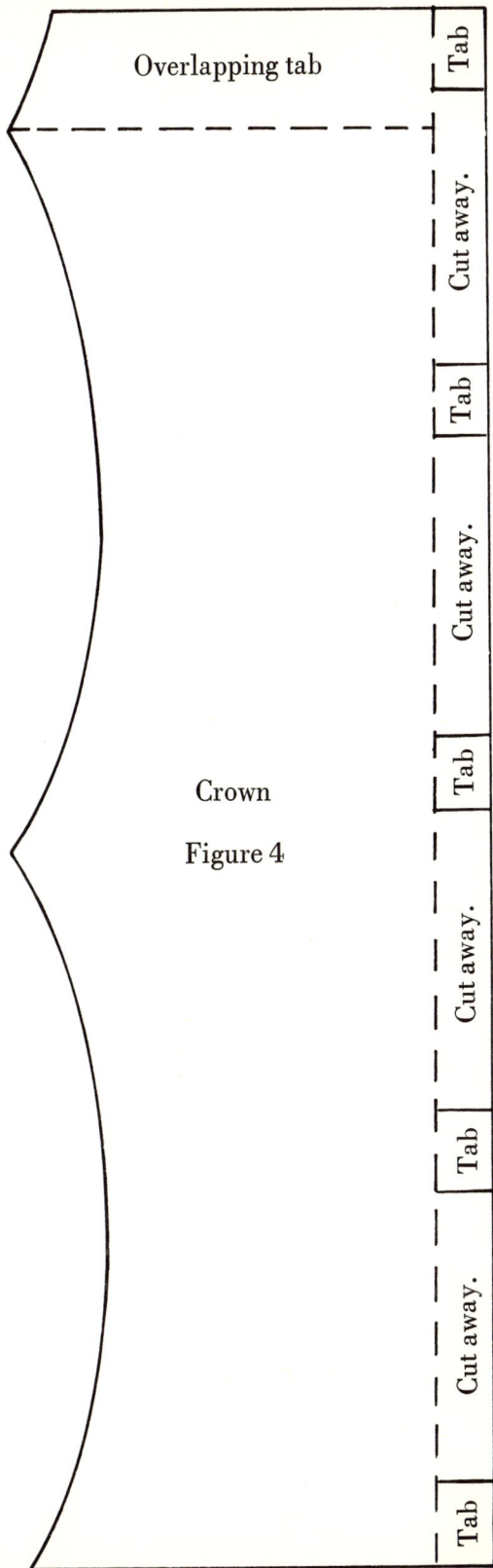

Crown

Figure 4

Tab

Cut away.

Tab

Cut away.

Tab

Cut away.

Trace and cut along solid lines.
Fold dotted line.

Figure 5

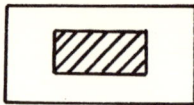

Buckle

Trace and cut solid lines.

Figure 6

Eye

Trace and cut solid lines.

Figure 7

Mouth

Cut both solid and
dotted lines.

9. Glue the white piece to the center of the lower part of the crown. Press to hold. Allow to dry. It should look like Figure 5.
10. Place hat snugly over puppet's head, and notice where it touches the head.
11. Dab glue around puppet's head at this place. Position hat over the head and press to hold. Allow to dry.
FACIAL FEATURES:
1. Trace Figure 6.
2. Transfer the pattern to black construction paper, holding it down with your finger. Cut out two.
3. Glue the eyes to the head and insert a straight pin. Press to hold. Allow to dry. Remove pins.
4. Cut out a small circle of black construction paper to make the nose. Glue it to the head, insert a straight pin, press to hold, allow to dry, and remove the pin.
5. Trace Figure 7 to make the mouth.
6. Place the pattern on black construction paper. Holding it down with your finger, trace it and cut it out.
7. Glue it to the face, insert a straight pin, press it in place until it dries, and remove the pin.

200

Back Opening

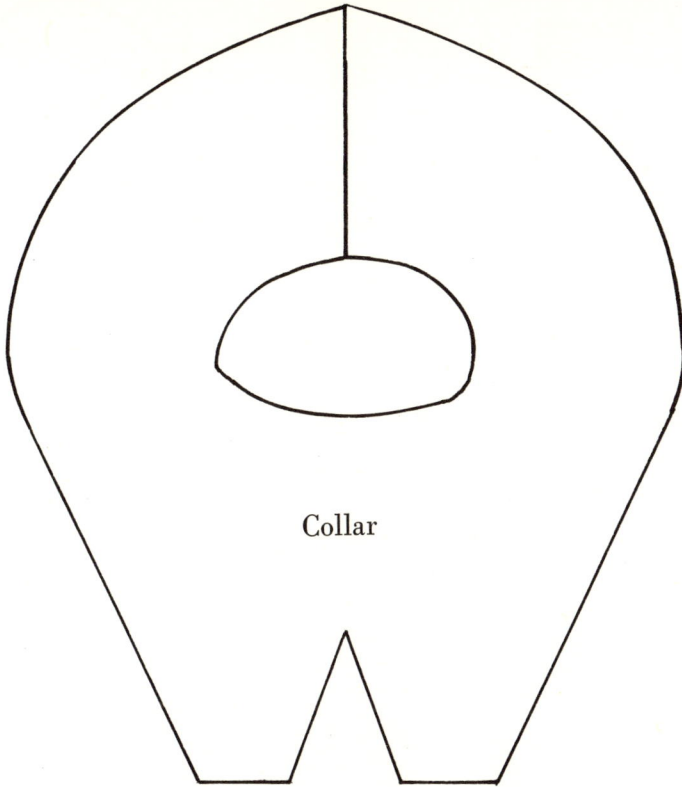

Collar

Figure 8

Trace and cut along solid lines.

COLLAR:

1. Trace Figure 8.

2. Transfer the pattern to white felt. Pin it in place and cut out the felt. Slash the back opening. Remove the pins and the pattern.

3. Drape the collar around the neck and tack it at the shoulders. Dab glue under the collar and hold it in place until it dries. White construction paper may be used instead of felt, but it is not as durable. If you do use construction paper, follow Steps 1 to 14 in the Tracing Directions.

201

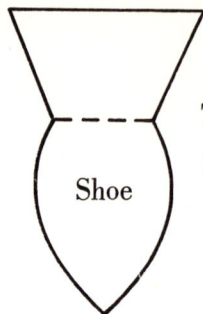

Trace and cut solid lines.

Fold dotted line.

Figure 9

SHOES:

1. Trace Figure 9.

2. Transfer the pattern to black construction paper and cut out two shoes.

3. Apply glue to the back of each flap.

4. Glue each flap against the front of the breeches, at the bottom. Hold them in place until the glue dries.

5. Make a shoe buckle the same way that you made the hat buckle (Steps 7 to 9 under HAT), but make it smaller and reverse the colors.

Suggestions for Other Pilgrim Puppets:

1. To make children, follow the directions for making the adults, but make them smaller. To distinguish the boys and girls from adults, eliminate hats and make the costumes in different colors.

2. You may want to make a papier-maché head instead of a stuffed-nylon-stocking head.

Holding the Puppet for Action:

1. Place your hand inside the tunic, behind the crepe-paper waist.

2. Place your index finger up through the neck tube and inside the head.

3. Insert your thumb through the tunic opening on one side, and your middle finger through opening on the other side.

202

4. Your thumb and middle fingers will become the puppet's arms and hands. Move your thumb and middle finger to make the puppet's arms and hands move. Use your index finger to move the head forward, backward, sideways. Bend your wrist to make your puppet bow and walk.

5. Practice your motions, looking at the puppet or watching it in a mirror to see how the movements will appear to the audience.

Production Notes

Scenery and Properties:

The play takes place in the interior of a Pilgrim's kitchen. A fireplace is painted on the backdrop, with a black pot hanging over the fire. On each side of the fireplace, there are two large windows through which the outdoors can be seen. A meat-turning spit is seen from one of the windows. The kitchen has a table with small paper plates, nuts, and foodstuffs. A list of chores is posted on a wall. There is also an open door at the side for William to look through as he counts the arriving guests. Puppets enter and exit from opposite sides of stage.

Action:

The excitement of this play is centered on the wonderful food that will shortly be enjoyed by the Pilgrims and a few invited Indian guests. When the Indians start arriving, loud shouts are heard from behind the stage. Excitement builds up when the Pilgrims realize that many more guests are arriving than were expected. When William starts counting them through the open door, there is a great deal of agitation, shown by movement and voice. As William counts the pitch of his voice rises, expressing disbelief. The ladies move about in a dither, looking through the windows to see how many guests are arriving. Just before the curtain closes, the women and girls embrace one another joyously.

CHRISTMAS

The Three Kings

L A U R A   R O S S

Long, long ago in a faraway land there lived three kings, Balthazar, the eldest, Melchior, middle-aged, and Caspar, the youngest. They were wise kings who knew how to read the messages flashed earthward by the stars in the heavens.

One night, while searching and scanning the sky together, they saw a new and strange star. It was brighter than any of the stars around it. Shafts of light radiated from it. King Balthazar was the first to discover it.

"Look!" he cried, facing eastward, "there is a strange star! Never before has there been such a star."

At this, King Melchior and King Caspar peered intently in the direction of the east. "It is, indeed, a strange star," said Melchior. "And how brightly it shines! What can it mean?"

Caspar, being the youngest, was most excited. "Perhaps," he said, "the star has come closer so its people can better see what our earthly kingdom is like."

"I think the star is trying to tell us that the crops of our people will be increased two-fold at the next harvest," said King Melchior.

205

Then old and wise Balthazar spoke, slowly and with great dignity. "It can mean only one thing. A new King has been born, directly beneath the shining light of this star. He is a great King, of all people, of all lands."

"Yes, yes," the others agreed. "That must be the message. A new-born King of all the lands. We must go immediately to see Him."

But Balthazar shook his head and said, "First we must prepare for our journey. See, the strange star is in the east. It will take many days to get there."

And so the three kings and their servants hastened to make ready for their journey. They labored all night. The cooks prepared delicious foods; the camel drivers washed and scrubbed their camels; clothing was gathered and packed; and tents were folded and made ready to be tied to the camels' backs.

In the midst of all the preparations, King Melchior suddenly said, "What gifts should we bring and lay before the new-born King?" But King Balthazar had not forgotten. "These too, are being made ready," he replied.

Three small chests, richly carved and covered with precious gems, were soon brought before the kings. One was filled with new gold, one with myrrh and one with frankincense.

At the break of dawn the caravan was ready to leave. At the command of their drivers, the camels knelt. Bags of food were placed on the backs of some; others carried packages of clothing and still others carried mounds of folded tents. King Melchior and King Caspar were ready to lead the caravan with their camels. In their hands they carried the chests of precious gifts. But King Balthazar was nowhere to be seen. "Where is Balthazar?" asked Caspar, looking around.

King Balthazar was walking about among the tents of the

people who were remaining behind. He was searching for something else.

"What is it that you are looking for?" called out Melchior. A small boy in ragged clothing was standing close by. He had bright, friendly eyes. Balthazar beckoned to the boy to come to him. The little boy walked hesitantly toward the king. He was afraid he had done some wrong to irritate the wise man. But Balthazar said, "We are going on a journey to see a new-born King. Come with us, for one day when you are older, you will be as wise as we and shall tell the world of the wondrous sight you have seen."

The little boy was delighted and clapped his hands with joy. Since he was the son of a camel driver, he loved to ride on the camel's back. "I will go and tell my father and prepare for the journey," the boy answered. Then he scampered away.

The three kings waited for the boy to return. They were impatient to start the long journey. The boy was slow to join them.

Melchior, who was becoming very uneasy, called out, "Let us be on our way."

So the three kings prepared to leave without the boy. First came Balthazar, then Melchior, then Caspar, one behind the other, leading the caravan of camels.

Presently the boy came into sight, still wearing his ragged clothing. He was leading a little fat puppy who was white with large black spots. The dog seemed as happy as his little master, for he leaped and frisked about.

The three kings were puzzled as the boy came close to them. "Why are you bringing the puppy?" asked Balthazar.

The little boy bent down and hugged his pet, for he loved him dearly, his only possession and companion. And then he said, "I too wish to bring a gift to the new-born King. My puppy is the only gift I have to give." Once again, with his arms around the puppy, he hugged him tightly to himself.

Then King Balthazar spoke in a very solemn voice: "We three kings bear gifts of great riches for the new-born King; gold, frankincense, and myrrh. But greater than these is the gift of love the child bears for the newly born babe."

With this, the caravan started on its journey to find the babe who was King of all the lands.

King Puppet

Materials:

Bristol board, white

decorative gift-wrap paper, or decorative upholstery or other fabric

gold or silver gift-wrap paper

narrow rod, 10 inches long

black knitting yarn or black crepe paper

Elmer's Glue-All

scissors

ruler

pencil

small lace doily

small silver stars (optional)

Directions:

BODY:

1. Make a 9 inch cone with Bristol paper (see Basic Shapes). Before gluing the cone, use it as a pattern to cut out a piece of gold gift-wrap paper. Place the gold paper over the Bristol paper. Roll both together into a cone with the gold paper on the outside. Glue the sides. Now you have a cone covered with gold paper.

HEAD:

1. Make a $4\frac{1}{2}$ inch cone with Bristol paper, using one half of an 8 inch diameter circle. When this cone is turned upside down, it should fit snugly into the top opening of the body cone.

2. Glue one end of the rod. Keeping the head cone upside down, insert 1 inch of the glued end of the rod into the inner side of the narrow opening. Press to hold and allow to dry. This becomes the holding rod for the head.

3. Insert the free end of the holding rod into the narrow opening of the body cone, and pull it down snugly. Be sure the holding rod aligns with the base of the body cone on the table. If necessary, trim it with a knife. The head cone, inverted, fits snugly into the body cone. The assembled king should look like Figure 1.

4. Measure and cut gold paper, 6 by 2 inches, to make the crown. Draw and cut zigzag lines on one 6 inch side. Fit the crown around the wide opening of the head cone. Glue the two edges together. Dab glue on the inner back side of the crown and slip it over the upper $\frac{1}{4}$ inch of the head cone. Hold it in place until it dries.

5. Add a beard, gluing several strands of black yarn to the chin and making them as long as desired. Narrow strips of black crepe paper may be used instead of yarn.

6. Draw and cut out a large letter "T" from black construction paper for the eyes and nose. Glue it on the face and hold it in place until it dries.

7. One strand of black yarn glued under the nose will serve as a mustache.

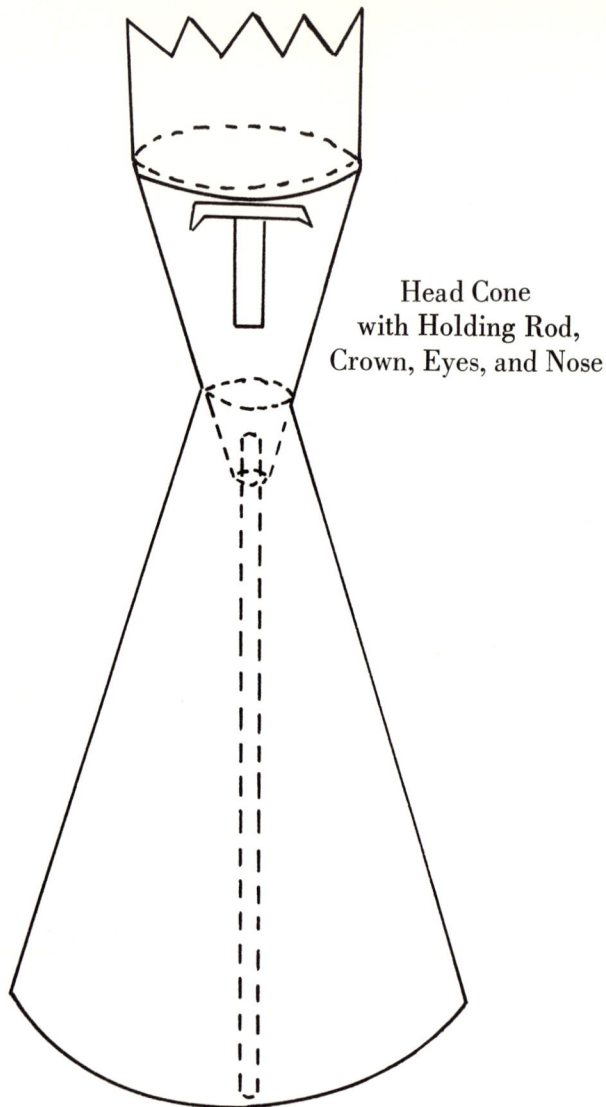

Head Cone
with Holding Rod,
Crown, Eyes, and Nose

Figure 1

Assembled King

COSTUME:

1. Remove the head cone from the body cone.

2. To make the robe, measure and cut a piece of decorative gift-wrap paper, 14 inches at the base, 10 inches at the top, and 9½ inches on the sides (see Figure 2).

Figure 2

3. Make three pleats on each 9½ inch side (see Paper Techniques).

4. Overlap the pleats at the tops of the right and left sides of the cloak and fit it snugly around the neck of the body cone.

5. If the cloak fits, staple overlapped pleats at the top of each side. If it is loose, pleat each side until it fits.

6. Apply glue around the neck of the body cone.

7. Attach the robe around the neck of the body, overlapping one side over the other snugly (Figure 3). Press to hold and allow to dry.

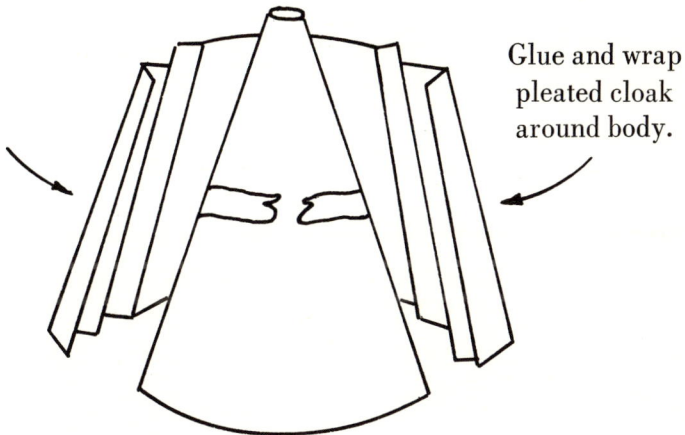

Glue and wrap pleated cloak around body.

Figure 3

8. For a collar, use a small round paper-lace doily. Cut a small hole in the center, large enough to fit over the top of the body cone. Slip it over the cone. Dab glue under the front and back of the doily and press it in place until it dries.

ARMS:

1. Cut an 8 by ½ inch strip of construction paper of any color. Fold it down the long side and glue the two sides together. Cut it in half for two 4 inch sturdy arms.

2. Draw and cut two small mittens from construction paper of the same color. Glue one to each arm. Press until it dries.

3. Curve the arms by pulling each one over the edge of the table. Apply glue to the straight end, and slip each arm under the cloak and around the body cone. Be sure the thumb of each mitten points up.

DECORATING KING:

1. Place the head cone with the holding rod back into the body cone.

2. Glue silver stars to each point of the crown.

3. For frankincense, myrrh, and gems, glue pieces of colored scrap paper, aluminum foil, small synthetic pearls, or sequins to the hands. If foil is used, it will not glue. Therefore, attach it by pushing a straight pin through each hand.

Suggestions for Making the Other Puppets in the Story:
1. Make the other kings the same way, using two inverted cones and a holding rod. You may use brown construction paper for the king's face.

2. The child and servants work best as hand puppets because of the action involved. Their heads can be made with a stuffed nylon stocking like the one in the Thanksgiving story. They can also be made with papier-maché. Instructions for holding a hand puppet appear in the Pilgrim Man project for the Thanksgiving story, entitled "Unexpected Guests."

3. Each king should be decorated differently. One may have a red beard, the other a brown or white beard. The crowns for each should also be constructed differently.

4. Robes should be decorated with different gift-wrap paper or fabric. Rickrack, gold, and silver braiding, or tassels may be attached to the front edges of the robe. Small gold or silver stars may be glued to the edges of the robe instead.

5. The camels that kneel may be made as jointed rod puppets with a large stuffed bag over their backs. See how to make and move this kind of puppet by referring to the Lincoln puppet. The stationary camels can be made simply as stick puppets, also with a large sack over their backs.

Holding the Puppet for Action:
Hold the bottom of body cone at the back with fingers of one hand. Twirl the holding rod with fingers of other hand. This will make the head move from side to side.

Dog Puppet

Materials:
white felt
brown and black fabric
cardboard
tracing paper
pencil
scissors
Elmer's Glue-All
four paper fasteners
two 9 inch rods

Directions:
1. Trace Figures 1 to 5 (see Tracing Directions). Place the

213

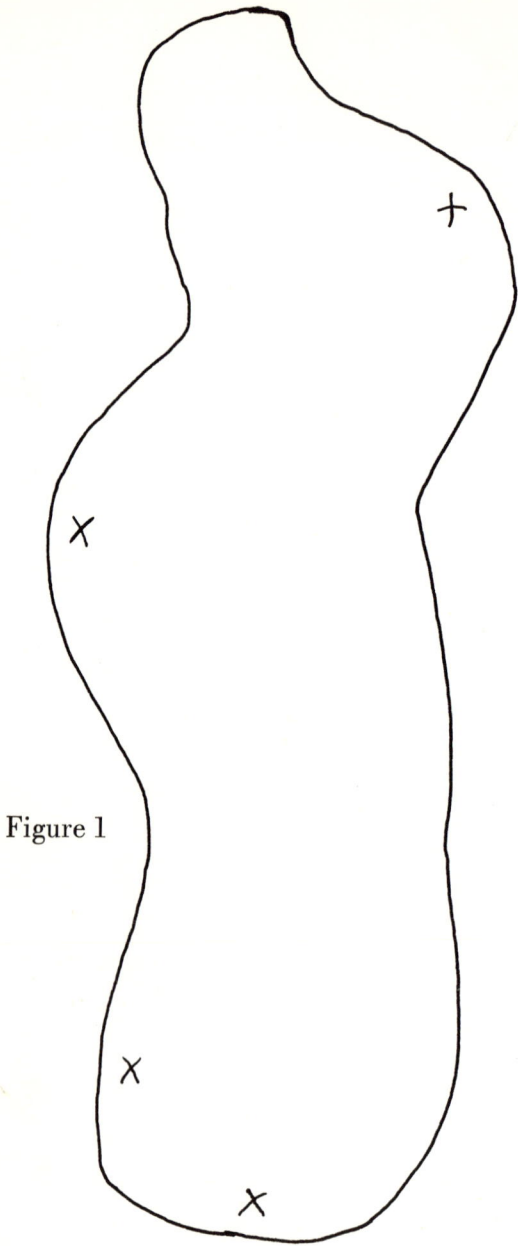

Figure 1

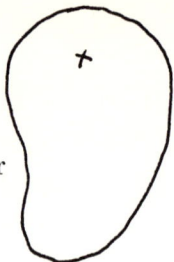

Ear

Figure 2

Foreleg

Figure 3

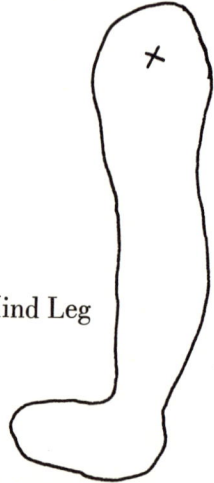

Hind Leg

Figure 4

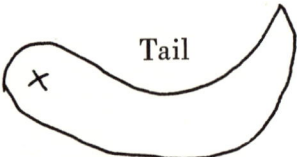

Tail

Figure 5

Toy Dog

Trace and cut out.   Attach to body
at points marked x.

patterns on cardboard. Hold them down with your fingers and outline in pencil. Remove the patterns and cut them out. These become templates (second patterns).

2. Place each template on white felt. Trace and cut out two pieces of felt for each foreleg, a total of four pieces of felt. Trace and cut out two pieces of felt for each hind leg, or four pieces of felt. Trace and cut out two pieces of felt for each ear, or four pieces of felt. Trace and cut two pieces of felt for the tail. Trace and cut two pieces of felt for the body.

3. Apply glue around the edge of each piece of felt and attach it to the corresponding template. Glue felt to each side of the legs, ears, body, and tail. Hold in place until it dries. Trim if necessary.

4. Place the forelegs together over a board and with a sharp tool, preferably the point of manicure scissors, make a hole through both legs at the place marked x in Figures 2 and 3. Make another hole at the attachment point on the body, as shown in Figure 6. Insert a paper fastener through the hole in one foreleg, through the hole in the fore part of the body, and through the hole in the second foreleg on the opposite side of the body. Secure the paper fastener. Now the front of the body separates the two forelegs.

5. Assemble the hind legs exactly the same way.

6. Attach the ears with the paper fasteners.

7. Add the tail, attaching it to one side of the body only. Make sure all paper fasteners face the same direction.

8. Cut out two small round pieces of black fabric for eyes. Cut smaller round pieces of white felt. Glue the white felt over the black fabric. Cut out two smaller round pieces of brown fabric. Glue them over the white felt. Glue one eye on each side of the dog's head.

9. To decorate the dog, cut irregular pieces of black fabric

215

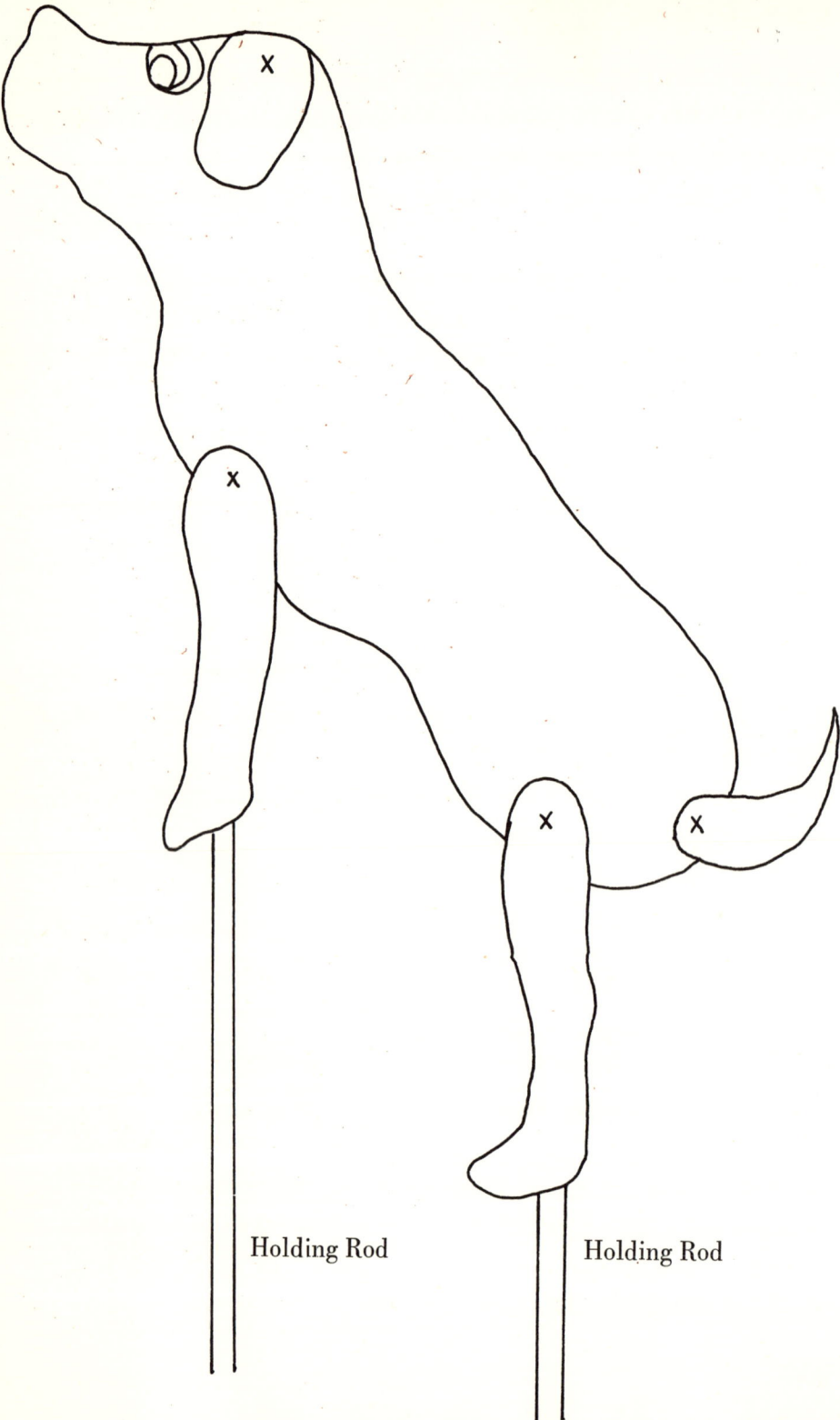

Holding Rod   Holding Rod

Assembled Toy Dog

and glue them to various places on the body, including the ears, both sides of the legs, and the tail.

Preparing the Puppet for Action:

1. With the point of a sharp tool, dig and scratch into the wood around one end of the rod.

2. Apply glue around this end and attach it between the inner lower part of the forelegs. Press to hold. Allow to dry.

3. Do the same for the hind legs.

Holding the Puppet for Action:

1. In a starting position, the rods are held parallel to each other, one in each hand.

2. In leaping, when the hind-leg rod is pushed up, the dog's hind legs are also pushed up, and the fore part of the dog's body comes down.

3. When the foreleg rod is pushed up, the dog's forelegs are pushed up, and the hind part of the body comes down.

4. Push rods as far up and down as the length of the dog's body will allow.

Production Notes

Techniques:

The best approach is to have a narrator read the story while the puppets pantomime. The narrator stands beside the stage or behind it. The presentation should be carefully synchronized, the actors performing while the narrator tells the story.

Scenery and Properties:

A distant scene painted on the backdrop represents the far-off land the three kings will travel to. A large bright star— possibly made of aluminum foil with shafts of light radiating from it—is attached to the scene. There are tents pitched here and there on the stage.

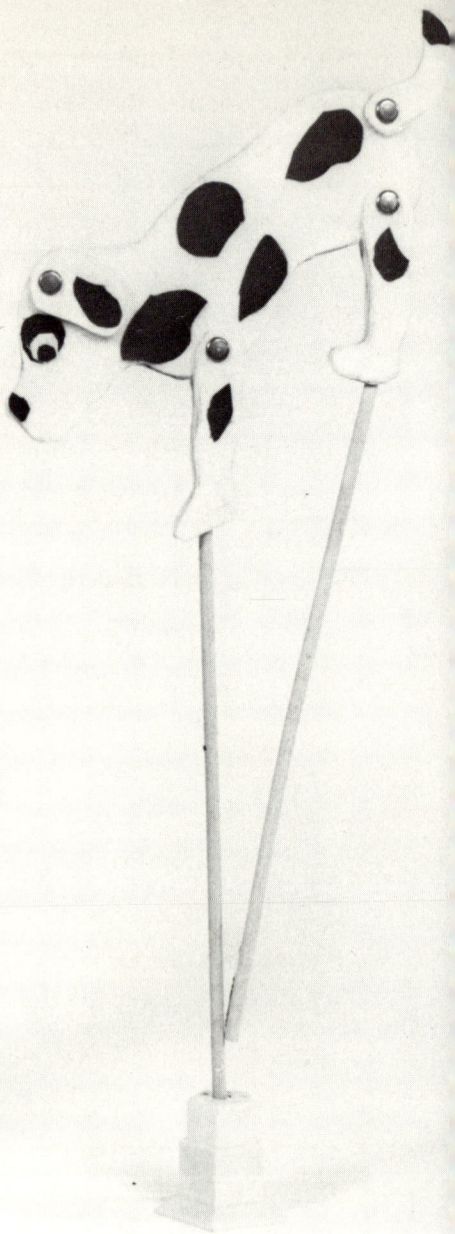

Action:

As the narrator reads the story, move the puppets to perform.
When a character speaks move the puppet's head slightly from

218

side to side. When the camels become impatient, simply move the stick-camel puppets back and forth.

When the child enters with the dog on stage, another puppeteer manipulates the rod puppet from below the stage. Keep the rods hidden below the stage so that the dog appears to be walking and leaping from the ground and not in midair. When the child laughs and claps his hands in the story, the narrator will make the sound effects. Be sure to show the action that goes on in preparing food, washing the camels, gathering clothing and folding tents, and also in placing these items on the camels' backs. Play the music of the Christmas carol, "We Three Kings Of Orient Are," as the caravan slowly makes its exit.

INDEX

ABOUT THE AUTHOR

Laura Ross, the author of Lothrop's well-received PUPPET
SHOWS USING POEMS AND STORIES, HAND PUPPETS: *How to
Make and Use Them*, and FINGER PUPPETS: *Easy to Make,
Fun to Use* is a former teacher and librarian who has worked
with children for years. Mrs. Ross has wide experience in
making puppets, producing shows, and writing original stories
for plays. She has also conducted puppet shows, and story-
hour and puppet-workshop programs in libraries. Mrs. Ross
is a member of the Long Island Puppet Guild and Puppeteers
of America and has appeared with her puppets on TV. She
lives in Southampton, New York with her writer husband,
Frank Ross, Jr.